Studies in
Classics

Edited by

Dirk Obbink
Oxford University

Andrew Dyck
The University of California,
Los Angeles

A Routledge Series

STUDIES IN CLASSICS
DIRK OBBINK AND ANDREW DYCK, *General Editors*

SINGULAR DEDICATIONS
Founders and Innovators of Private Cults in Classical Greece
Andrea L. Purvis

EMPEDOCLES
An Interpretation
Simon Trépanier

APHRODITE AND EROS
The Development of Greek Erotic Mythology
Barbara Breitenberger

RHETORIC IN CICERO'S *PRO BALBO*
An Interpretation
Kimberly Anne Barber

"FOR SALVATION'S SAKE"
Provincial Loyalty, Personal Religion, and Epigraphic Production in the Roman and Late Antique Near East
Jason Moralee

AMBITIOSA MORS
Suicide and Self in Roman Thought and Literature
Timothy D. Hill

A Linguistic Commentary on Livius Andronicus

Ivy Livingston

Taylor & Francis Group
NEW YORK AND LONDON

Published in 2004 by
Routledge
Taylor & Francis Group
711 Third Avenue
New York, NY 10017

Published in Great Britain by
Routledge
Taylor & Francis Group
2 Park Square,
Milton Park, Abingdon,
Oxfordshire OX14 4RN

First issued in paperback 2014

Routledge is an imprint of the Taylor and Francis Group, an informa business

Copyright © 2004 by Taylor & Francis Group, a Division of T&F Informa.

All rights reserved. No part of this book may be reprinted or reproduced or utilized in any form or by any electronic, mechanical, or other means, now known or hereafter invented, including photocopying and recording, or in any information storage or retrieval system, without permission in writing from the publishers.

ISBN 13: 978-0-415-96899-7 (hbk)
ISBN 13: 978-0-415-86143-4 (pbk)

Catalog record is available from the Library of Congress

Parentibus

et

Praeceptoribus

Contents

Series Editors' Foreword	ix
Preface by Michael Weiss	xi
Acknowledgments	xxi
Introduction	1
Commentary*	
Section One: The Odyssey	
2 *fīlie*, 5 *Laertie*	5
10 *Morta*	7
15 *nequīnont*, 36 *inserinuntur*	13
25, 33, 34 *topper*	17
30 *Monētās*	23
33 *homōnēs*	31
39 *gāvīsī*	37
40 *pulla*	39
41 *mandisset*	41
46 *dextrābus*	43
Section Two: Tragedies	
4 *praeda*	47
20 *opēs, opitulā*	57
29 *praestōlārās*	61
38 *nefrendem, lacteam inmulgens opem*	67
Conclusion	71
Appendix	73
Bibliography	83
Index	85

* The numbering of the fragments follows Warmington, *Remains of Old Latin*.

Series Editors' Foreword

Studies in Classics aims to bring high-quality work by emerging scholars to the attention of a wider audience. Emphasizing the study of classical literature and history, these volumes contribute to the theoretical understanding of human culture and society over time. This series will offer an array of approaches to the study of Greek and Latin (including medieval and Neolatin), authors and their reception, canons, transmission of texts, ideas, religion, history of scholarship, narrative, and the nature of evidence.

While the focus is on Mediterranean cultures of the Greco-Roman era, perspectives from other areas, cultural backgrounds, and eras are to be included as important means to the reconstruction of fragmentary evidence and the exploration of models. The series will reflect upon the role classical studies has played in humanistic endeavors from antiquity to the present, and explore select ways in which the discipline can bring both traditional scholarly tools and the experience of modernity to bear on questions and texts of enduring importance.

Dirk Obbink, Oxford University
Andrew Dyck, The University of California, Los Angeles

Preface

Michael Weiss
Cornell University

The facts and not-quite-facts about Livius Andronicus, his life and works are available in any number of reliable handbooks, but for convenience I will rehearse them here.[1]

Date

According to Cicero (*Brutus* 72–73), who names Atticus and *antiqui commentarii* as his sources, Livius first presented a play in the consulship of C. Claudius Ap. f. Centho and M. Sempronius C. f. Tuditanus (240 BCE). Cicero sticks to the same date at *Tusc.* 1.3[2] and *Cato* 50.[3] And indeed this date is followed by most later scholars both ancient and modern.[4] But Cicero also reports that Livius' dates were a subject of debate because Accius claimed that Livius was captured from Tarentum in the fifth consulship of Quintus Maxumus (209 BCE). Further Accius reported that he produced a play in 197 BCE during the consulship of C. Cornelius and Q. Minucius at the *Ludi Iuventatis*, which M. Livius Salinator had vowed to establish at the battle of Sena in 207 BCE.[5] This later chronology seems to have been followed by Suetonius since it makes an appearance in Jerome's chronology, but it has found few modern supporters.[6] Cicero claims that Accius' chronology is wrong because it would make Livius, supposedly the first to put on a play, younger than Plautus and Naevius. It is obvious that Cicero's argument is a *petitio principii* since we do not know what dates Accius would have attributed to Plautus and Naevius. Whatever the exact dates of Livius Andronicus, it is clear that the native tradition regarded him as the initiator of Latin literary production.[7]

Name

In the ancient sources Livius Andronicus is generally referred to as just Livius. The cognomen Andronicus appears for the first time in Quintilian, although Festus p. 446.32 L following Verrius Flaccus allows us to trace the second name back at least to the Augustan period.[8] Given standard Roman naming practice for freedmen it is plausible that Andronicus might represent the author's original Greek name and Livius the gentilicium of his patron and quondam owner, reported in some sources to have been M. Livius Salinator.[9] The praenomen is given as L. by Aulus Gellius and Cassiodorus but as T. by Jerome, which presumably is the result of confusion with the much more famous T. Livius.[10]

Origin

Cicero reports that Accius wrote that Livius was captured from Tarentum.[11] Although this fact is embedded in a chronology that is not usually found credible, many scholars have accepted it. However, while it is true that Roman influence and hegemony had begun in Tarentum by the end of the Pyrrhic war in 272, the city was not captured nor its people enslaved. So while the Tarentine origin of Livius can be easily fitted into the high chronology, it is harder to understand how Livius could have come to Rome as a war-captive. Suetonius (*De Grammaticis et Rhetoribus* 1) refers to him along with Ennius as *semigraecus*. It is, of course, evident from his work that he was familiar with Greek and this may be all we can say with certainty.

Livius' Status and Employment

Suetonius reports that like Ennius Livius is known to have taught both Greek and Latin privately and publicly at Rome. Suetonius' claim that they merely clarified the meaning of Greek authors and gave readings from their own Latin compositions is presumably an inference based on grammatical practice in his day.[12] Jerome, relying on Suetonius' *De Poetis,* adds another detail about Livius' teaching duties and servile status: Livius Salinator freed the poet Livius, who had been his children's instructor, *ob ingenii meritum* in the year 188/7. Since the date given agrees with Accius' chronology it is conceivable that Suetonius drew this information directly or indirectly from that author.[13] The association of Livius Andronicus and Livius Salinator in Jerome seems to confirm this since the Accius passage dates a play of Livius to the *Ludi Iuventatis* of 197 BCE, which had been vowed by Livius Salinator at the battle of Sena in 207 BCE. It is conceivable that the two dates for Livius Andronicus' *floruit* result from a confusion of Livii Salinatores. Most scholars believe that the Salinator who freed Livius was the M. Livius Salinator, recorded as *magister Xvir.* of the fictive *Ludi Saeculares* of 236 BCE in the *Fasti Capitolini*.[14] This Livius Salinator was the father of the famous M. Livius Salinator consul and dictator, and the grandfather of C. Livius Salinator consul of 188.[15] It is conceivable that Accius's dating, if indeed erroneous, results from a confusion of the *decemvir* with the homonymous consul of 219 and 207. Of course it is also just possible that the entire association with the Livii Salinatores has been fabricated on the basis of the gentilic Livius and that the association of M. Livius Salinator the elder with the *Ludi Saeculares*, celebrated in Rome at the place in the Campus Martius called Tarentum/Terentum, led to the connection of Livius with the homonymous city of Magna Graecia.[16]

Literary Career and Works

To Livius are attributed dramatic works, a hymn and a translation of the Odyssey. The first play was staged in 240 BCE, the year after the end of the first Punic war. Livy in his famous account of the origins of drama at Rome (7.2.8) recounts how Livius was the first to create a *fabula* with a plot (*argumentum*). Further Livy relates that upon straining his voice Livius, who was himself an actor, left the singing to a professional and gesticulated in a livelier fashion since he was not bothered with having to sing himself. From that time on actors limited themselves to dialogue portions only (*diverbia*).[17]

The following tragic titles are known: *Achilles, Aegisthus, Aiax Mastigophorus, Andromeda, Antiopa, Danae, Equos Troianus, Hermiona, Tereus*.[18]

Festus preserves six fragments that are attributed to comedies. Two titles, *Gladiolus* and *Ludius*, are certain but a third, *Virgo*, is probably corrupt. Livius was also said to have composed a hymn for a chorus of twenty-seven maidens for an expiatory rite of 207.[19] For the success of this hymn and the rite it formed a part of, a *collegium scribarum histrionumque* was established in Livius' honor in the temple of Minerva on the Aventine, where actors and writers could gather and offer gifts.[20]

Most famously of all, Livius translated the Odyssey into Saturnians.[21] At what stage in his career and for what reasons he undertook this task is unknown. The frequently repeated idea that Livius' *Odysseia*[22] was intended as a school-text is unsupported by any direct ancient testimony. Of course the well-known passage *Ep.* 2.1.69–71 shows that some of Livius did become a school-text, much to Horace's regret.[23]

Meter

While the dramatic works are written in meters adapted from Greek, the iambic *senarius* and the trochaic *septenarius*, the *Odyssia* is written in the apparently native and famously problematic Saturnian. It is unlikely that Livius Andronicus himself was solely responsible for the adaptation of Greek dramatic meters. As Fraenkel has pointed out, the innovations distinguishing even Livius' Latin *senarii* and *septenarii* from their Greek models are not likely to be the work of just a single lifetime. Furthermore, the so-called *versus quadratus*, itself based on Greek models, appears to have been long adapted to popular non-literary use.[24] Finally, it has recently been claimed that the South Picene metrical inscriptions dating from the 5th century BCE make use of Greek-derived meters.[25]

On the other hand, no serious attempt has been made in modern times to trace the Saturnian to Greek sources and the principles of its scansion remain controversial to the present day.[26] It is, however, common to Latin and the Sabellic languages, but whether this commonality is to be explained as the result of shared inheritance from Proto-Italic or metrical diffusion within the Italic cultural *koiné* is unclear.[27]

The Work in Question

The majority of scholarship on Livius Andronicus has traditionally been strictly philological or literary-historical. In particular, much work has focussed on the relationship between Livius' translations and their Greek originals.[28]

The one full-scale study devoted specifically to the language of Livius is the unpublished University of Minnesota dissertation completed in 1975 by Gabriele Erasmi, *Studies on the Language of Livius Andronicus*. This gigantic work, a storehouse of useful information, includes a descriptive grammar of the fragments and detailed studies of the Livian onomasticon. The present monograph, however, has a different focus. Since the meager fragments of Livius represent our earliest—or nearly earliest—literary Latin they provide valuable evidence for the language before the heavy hand of Latin literary tradition led to morphological and syntactic streamlining. By interrogating the fragments from the point of view of historical and Indo-European linguistics one may hope to gain insight into the pre-history of Latin and the initial development of the Latin literary tradition. In the 1997 dissertation of Ivy Livingston, Livian forms are the starting points for far-reaching discussions of Latin historical phonology and morphology. Among the most interesting results are the elucidation of the prehistory of the vocatives of *-iįo-*stems, the class of deverbal nouns in *-ētum* and *-ēta*, the prehistory of the paradigm of *homo*, and the etymology and morphology of *praeda* and *praestolari*. In an appendix a new and plausible theory for the origin of the Latin adjective in *-ulentus* is offered.

Addenda and Corrigenda

Pg. 3

The Umbrian forms **heris** and **heri** are not the best examples for the fourth conjugation in Umbrian since they could well be optative forms, either *$heri$- or $her\bar{\imath}$-. A clearer example in Umbrian would be **amparitu** 'stand' (tr.).

The analogically remade vocative in *-$i\underset{\smile}{i}e$ is reflected also in Oscan **statie** (CM 18 = Vett. 110).

Pg. 12–13

The avoidance of monosyllables as a motivation for innovation has been studied in detail by Löfstedt 1956:35–62.

Pg. 36n3

Ved. *ávati* is perhaps better taken with Latin *iuvo* not *aveo*. See LIV^2:243.

Pg. 39

Warmington *Od.* 41 is one of the four hexameters attributed to Livius Andronicus. Presumably they date to a later post-Ennian reworking of the *Odyssia*. For other possible reconstructions of the root behind *mando* see LIV^2:442.

Pg. 53–54

The connection of *opus* with *epulum* is dubious. There is no reason to think that an *epulum* was originally only a religious banquet nor for that matter that *opus* and its cognates have any particular sacral/cultic connection. Vedic *ápas* is a hapax of uncertain meaning. I would prefer to derive *epulum* from the root *h_1ep- 'take.' For the semantics cf. Serbian and Croatian *ručak* 'meal' < – *ručati* 'take (a meal).' If one does not connect *epulum* and *opus* then there is no formal difficulty in connecting both *opus ops* with PIE *h_3ep-. The semantics, however, require further elucidation.

Concordance of Fragments Treated

Warmington *Od.* 2 = Blänsdorf 2
Warmington *Od.* 5 = Blänsdorf 4
Warmington *Od.* 10 = Blänsdorf 23
Warmington *Od.* 15 = Blänsdorf 11

Warmington *Od.* 23–26 = Blänsdorf 18
Warmington *Od.* 30 = Blänsdorf 21
Warmington *Od.* 33 = Blänsdorf 25
Warmington *Od.* 34 = Blänsdorf 24
Warmington *Od.* 35–36 = Blänsdorf 34
Warmington *Od.* 39 = Blänsdorf 22
Warmington *Od.* 40 = Blänsdorf 27
Warmington *Od.* 41 = Blänsdorf 39
Warmington *Od.* 46 = Blänsdorf 29

Abbreviations

DNP = *Der Neue Pauly Enkyklopädie der Antike* edited by Hubert Cancik and Helmuth Schneider, Stuttgart Weimar, 1996.

DKP = *Der Kleine Pauly Lexikon der Antike* edited by Konrat Ziegler and Walther Sontheimer, Munich, 1975.

GLK = *Grammatici latini* ex recensione Henrici Keilii, Leipzig, 1857–1880.

LIV^2 = *Lexikon der indogermanischen Verben*, second edition, edited by Helmut Rix, Wiesbaden, 2001.

OCD^3 = *Oxford Classical Dictionary*, third edition, edited by Simon Hornblower and Antony Spawforth, Oxford and New York, 1996.

RE = *Paulys Real-encyclopädie der classischen Altertumswissenschaft*. Neue bearbeitung, edited by G. Wissowa, Stuttgart, 1894–.

NOTES

1. See especially Suerbaum 2002:93–104, OCD^3:876–877 (Jocelyn); DNP:7:373–378 (Suerbaum) DKP:3:692–695 (Mariotti); RE Suppl. V:598–607 (Fraenkel). Thanks to Rip Cohen, Michelle Kwintner and Alan Nussbaum for advice and commentary.
2. *Annis fere CCCCX post Romam conditam Livius fabulam dedit C. Claudio, Caeci filio, M.Tuditano consulibus anno ante natum Ennium, qui fuit maior natu quam Plautus et Naevius.*
3. *Vidi (i.e. Cato) etiam senem Livium; qui cum sex annis ante quam ego natus sum, fabulam docuisset Centone Tuditanoque consulibus, usque in aduluscentiam meam processit aetate.*
4. Gellius 17.21.42 probably following Varro.
5. However, Livy 36.36.4 dates these games to 191.
6. Hier. *chron.* a. Abr. 1829/30 = 188/187 *T. Livius tragoediarum scriptor clarus habetur, qui ob ingenii meritum a Livio Salinatore, cuius liberos erudiebat, libertate donatus est.* For the Suetonian origin of this passage see Kaster 1995:49. Valerius Antias *apud* Livy 36.36.4 also may have been following Accius' chronology since he

dates the first theatrical performances to the *Megalesia* of 191 BCE, the same year as the celebration of Livius Salinator's *Ludi Iuventatis* according to Livy. The most notable modern defenders of Accius are Mattingly 1957 and 1971 and Marconi 1966.
7. At least as the founder of Roman theater: Horace *Ep*. 2.1.62 with Schol. Hor. Γ *qui primus comoedias scripsit*; Livy 7.2.8–10; Aulus Gellius 17.21 *primus omnium L. Livius poeta fabulas docere Romae coepit*; Val. Max. 2.4.4; Gloss. Lat. Ansil. p. 128, s.v. *comoedia*; Diom. GLK 1.489.7; Euanthius *com.* 4.3. As first poet: Quinitilian *Inst.* 10.2.7 *nihil in poetis supra Livium Andronicum*.
8. It is also found in Aulus Gellius 18.9.5, Priscian GLK II 208, 301, 305.8, 321.6, the Schol. Hor. Γ, Gloss. Lat. Ansil., Diom. and Gloss. Lat. Ansil. passages quoted in fn. 7 and the Old Church Slavonic translation of a work attributed to Rhetorius.
9. However, it is noteworthy that inscriptions prior to 100 BCE do not record the cognomen of a freedman. See Gordon 1935. If the cognomen *Andronicus* has any validity in this case it must have been preserved in some other fashion.
10. Aulus Gellius 17.21 quoted above in fn. 7. Cassiodorus *chron.* II 128 M. 316: *C. Manlius et Q. Valerius. His consulibus* (239 BCE) *ludis Romanis primum tragoedia et comoedia a L. Livio ad scaenam data*.
11. Ἀνδρόνικος is a common name in the Hellenistic period, but for what it's worth it is attested for Tarentum by *Fouilles de Delphes* III (4) 427 III.1 (205–203 BCE). Note, by the way, that Accius says that Livius was captured from Tarentum. That he was a native of the same place is merely an inference.
12. See Kaster 1995:54.
13. Note, however, that Beare 1940 has questioned Livius' servile status. He suggests that Livius' servile status may be an inference of imperial date.
14. See Broughton 1951–2:1.223.
15. See Broughton 1951–2:1.236, 294, 365.
16. A different reconstruction in Palmer 1974:96 who amalgamates the *decemvir* and the consul.
17. The controversies of this passage are many and the bibliography is enormous. See the sampling offered by Oakley 1998:40.
18. See Suerbaum 2002:98 for more details about the probable Greek sources for these plays.
19. Livy 27.36.3–4; Festus 446.26 L s.v. *scribas*. Suerbaum 2002:99 suggests that the statement of Serv. auct. ad *Aen. 4.37 Livius autem Andronicus refert eos (sc. Afros) de Romanis saepius triumphasse suasque porticus Romanis spoliis adornasse* may be derived from this hymn.
20. Festus p. 446, 448 L. On this *collegium* and its relationship to the *collegium poetarum* mentioned by Valerius Maximus 3.7.11 see Horsfall 1976.
21. Suerbaum 1992 argues that the translation must have been much abbreviated.
22. This spelling is the only one authoritatively transmitted. The frequent spelling *Odusia* is a restored archaic spelling not directly attested.
23. *Non equidem insector delendaue carmina Liui/esse reor, memini quae plagosum mihi paruo/Orbilium dictare*. An Old Church Slavonic translation of a lost Greek work attributed to Rhetorius mentions Livius Andronicus in a hemerological context. See Beneševič 1925. Pingree 1977:223 doubts the attribution of the OCS text to Rhetorius.

24. See Fraenkel 1927 and Gerick 1996. See also Rix 1989 for arguments for the antiquity of iambic shortening.
25. Eichner 1990.
26. The most recent theory is put forth in Parsons 1999.
27. See Poccetti 1983. A probable Etruscan example of the *versus quadratus* is found on the 4th century BCE mirror from Volterra: *eca sren tva/ i xnac hercle / unial clan / θ[u]ra sce*. 'This image shows how Hercules became the son of Uni.' See Gerick 1996:19.
28. In particular Fränkel 1932; Mariotti 1952; Traina 1953; Verrusio 1942; Broccia 1974; Büchner 1979; Sheets 1981; Kearns 1990.

REFERENCES

Beneševič 1925: W. Beneševič, "Spuren des Werke des Ägypter Rhetorios, des Livius Andronicus und des Ovidius in altslavischer Übersetzung," *Byzantinische Zeitschrift*, 25 (1925) 310–312.

Beare 1940: William Beare, "When Did Livius Andronicus Come to Rome?" *Classical Quarterly*, 34 (1940) 11–19.

Blänsdorf 1995: Jürgen Blänsdorf, *Fragmenta poetarum latinorum epicorum et lyricorum praeter Ennium et Lucilium* post W. Morel novis curis adhibitis edidit Carolus Buechner editionem tertiam auctam curavit Jürgen Blänsdorf, Stuttgart and Leipzig, 1995.

Broccia 1974: Giuseppe Broccia, *Ricerche su Livio Andronico epico*, Padua, 1974.

Broughton 1951–2: T. Robert S. Broughton, *The Magistrates of the Roman Republic*, with the collaboration of Marcia L. Patterson. New York, 1951–52.

Büchner 1979: Karl Büchner, "Livius Andronicus und die erste künstlerische Übersetzung der europäischen Kultur," *Symbolae Osloenses*, 54 (1979) 37–70.

Eichner 1990: Heiner Eichner, "Ein Heldendenkmal der Sabiner mit trochäischen Epigramm eines pikenischen Plautus des fünften Jahrhunderts v. Chr.," *Sprache* 34 (1988–1990), 198–206.

Erasmi 1975: Gabriele Erasmi, *Studies on the Language of Livius Andronicus*, unpublished dissertation, University of Minnesota, 1975.

Fränkel 1932: Hermann Fränkel, "Griechische Bildung in altrömischen Epen," *Hermes*, 67 (1932) 598–607.

Fraenkel 1927: Eduard Fraenkel, "Die Vorgeschichte des *versus quadratus*," *Hermes*, 62 (1927) 357–370. Reprinted in *Kleine Beiträge zur klassischen philologie*, Vol. 2, Rome, 1964, 11–24.

Gerick 1996: Thomas Gerick, *Der* versus quadratus *bei Plautus und seine volkstümliche Tradition*, Tübingen, 1996.

Gordon 1935: Arthur E. Gordon, *Ephigraphica, I. On the First Appearance of the Cognomen in Latin Inscriptions of Freedmen, University of California Publications in Classical Archaeology* 1.4, 1935.

Horsfall 1976: Nicholas Horsfall "The *Collegium Poetarum*," *Bulletin of the Institute of Classical Studies*, 23 (1976) 79–95.

Kaster 1995: Robert A. Kaster, *C. Suetonius Tranquillus De Grammaticis et Rhetoribus*, edited with a translation, introduction, and commentary, Oxford, 1995.

Kearns 1990: John Michael Kearns, "Σεμνότης and Dialect Gloss in the Odussia of Livius Andronicus,"*American Journal of Philology*, 111 (1990) 40–52.
Löfstedt 1956: Einar Löfstedt, *Syntactica; Studien und Beiträge zur historischen Syntax des Lateins*, second edition, Vol. 2, Lund, 1956.
Mariotti 1952: Scevola Mariotti, *Livio Andronico e la traduzione artistica. Saggio critico ed edizione dei frammenti*, 1952, second edition 1986.
Marconi 1966: G. Marconi, *La cronologia di Livio Andronico*. Accademia Nazionale dei Lincei, 1966, (Memorie: Cl. di scienze mor. stor. e fil., Ser. 8, 12, 1966, 125–213.
Mattingly 1957: Harold B. Mattingly, "The Date of Livius Andronicus," *Classical Quarterly* n.s. 7 (1957), 158–163.
Mattingly 1971: Harold B. Mattingly, " Review of Marconi 1966," *Gnomon*, 43 (1971) 680–687.
Oakley 1998: Stephen P. Oakley, *A Commentary on Livy Books VI-X. Volume II. Books VII-VIII*, Oxford, 1998.
Palmer 1974: Robert E. A. Palmer, *Roman Religion and Roman Empire. Five Essays*, Philadelphia, 1974.
Parsons 1999: Jed Parsons, "A New Approach to the Saturnian Verse and its Relation to Latin Prosody," *Transactions of the American Philological Society*, 129 (1999) 117–137.
Pingree 1977: David Pingree, "Antiochus and Rhetorius," *Classical Philology*, 72 (1977) 203–223.
Poccetti 1983: Paolo Poccetti, "Eine Spur des saturnischen Verses im Oskischen," *Glotta*, 61 (1983) 207–217.
Rix 1989: Helmut Rix, "Dichtersprachliche Tradition aus vorliterarischer Zeit?" in *Studien zur vorliterarische Periode im frühen Rom*, ed. by Gregor Vogt-Spira, Tübingen, 1989.
Sheets 1981: George A. Sheets, "The Dialect Gloss, Hellenistic Poetics and Livius Andronicus," *American Journal of Philology*, 102 (1981) 58–78.
Suerbaum 1992: Werner Suerbaum, "Zum Umfang der Bücher in der archaischen lateinischen Dichtung: Naevius, Ennius, Lukrez und Livius Andronicus auf Papyrus-Rollen," *Zeitschrift für Papyrologie und Epigraphik*, (1992) 92, 53–173.
Suerbaum 2002: *Die Archaische Literatur von den Anfängen bis Sullas Tod*, edited by Werner Suerbaum, *Handbuch der lateinischen Literatur der Antike*, Vol. 1, Munich, 2002.

Acknowledgments

I would like to thank Professor Michael Weiss and Professor Brent Vine for their very generous comments and advice on various portions of this dissertation. The suggestions and questions of Professor Judith Ginsburg and Dr. Melanie Stowell helped, I hope, to improve its accessibility. Professor Andrew Dyck provided comments which aided immeasurably in the revision of this work for publication. To Professor Jay Jasanoff and, above all, Professor Alan Nussbaum, I owe a debt that cannot be calculated, only gratefully acknowledged. Any remaining errors of fact or judgment are, of course, my own fault.

Introduction

Although several editions of some or all of the fragments of Livius Andronicus have appeared within the last century, they contain little commentary. Also, virtually all recent major work on Livius, such as that of Mariotti, has focused on assessing his artistic talents and his ability as a translator of Homer. But, as the oldest literary Latin preserved in any quantity, the language of Livius shows many features of linguistic interest, as well, and raises many questions of phonology and morphology and a few of syntax. Therefore, I have undertaken to write a linguistic commentary on the text of Livius Andronicus.

This work is not, nor is it meant to be, exhaustive. For example, some features of archaic Latin that are linguistically significant, but perfectly well treated in the standard handbooks, are dealt with cursorily, if at all, here. Finally, although Livius provides the starting-point of each comment (organized by fragment, cited according to the text of Warmington), his language does not appear to differ significantly from that of his nearest successors, such as Naevius or Ennius, and hence many of the discussions do not also end with Livius, but explore wider-ranging problems of Latin and, to some degree, of Indo-European linguistics.

Section One:

The Odyssey

2
fīlie
5
Laertie

Od. 2 W: *'Pater noster, Saturni filie,*
Od. 5 W: '... *Neque enim te oblitus sum Laertie noster,*

Livius preserves these examples of *i̯o*-stem vocative singulars in *-ĭe̯ (-i̯ĕ)*, for classical *-ī*.[1] One would certainly expect the voc. sg. of a *i̯o*-stem to have been *-i̯ĕ* (cf., e.g., Gk. ὄλβιε[2]), parallel to the *-ĕ* of the *o*-stems. Thus *-ī* would appear to be some sort of treatment of earlier *-i̯ĕ*.

There is some evidence to show that *-ī-* was the regular development of *-i̯ĕ(-)* in open syllables in Latin. Several places in the paradigm of denominatives in *-i̯ᵉ/ₒ-* from *i*-stems (such as *fīnīre* 'to delimit' from *fīnis* 'limit') would have had this sequence. For example, the second and third singular of *fīnīre* would go back to forms of the shape **-i̯esi* and **-i̯eti*, which gave *fīnīs* and, prior to the regular shortening of vowels before a final *-t*, *fīnīt*.

If we compare the present of the fourth conjugation in Oscan and Umbrian, we also find *-ī(-)* from *-i̯ĕ(-)* in open syllables–for example Umbr. 2 sg. **heris**, 3 sg. **heri** and Osc. 3 sg. **sakruvit**. Thus, it can be concluded that this treatment was of Italic date. But if *-i̯ĕ(-)* gave *-ī(-)* already in proto-Italic, Old Latin cannot still have vocatives of the type *fīlie*. These forms cannot, therefore, be genuine archaisms, but rather have been analogically restored on the model of the *o*-stems (nom. sg. *-o-s* : voc. sg. *-ĕ* :: nom. sg. *-i̯o-s-* : voc. sg. *-X = -i̯ĕ*). Umbrian has reintroduced the "regular" ending as well, to judge from such forms as *arsie* 'sancte' and *Grabovie*, according to the same analogical model.

There is some evidence to suggest that, in Latin at least, *-ī-* is also the phonologically regular outcome of **-i̯V̆-* in open syllables, when the short vowel is **-ŏ-*, **-ă-*, or **-ŭ-*.

In the case of **i̯o-*, the first person plural of the fourth conjugation might show this treatment, e.g., *fīnīmus* < **-i̯ŏ-*. It is impossible, however, to guarantee that the stem vowel of *fīnīmus* has not simply been influenced by the second and third singular and second plural forms, in which the *-ī-* is from **-i̯ĕ-*. If **-i̯ŏ-mos* had given something other than *-ī-mus*, the paradigm could certainly have been leveled and *-īmus* introduced on the model of 2 sg. *-ās*, 3 sg. **-at* (> **-ă+*), 2 pl. **-ātis*, beside 1 pl. *-āmus*.

There appears to be better evidence, however, that *-i̯i̯ŏ-, like *-i̯i̯ĕ-, gave -ī- in open syllables. Oscan and Umbrian have a class of verbal nouns with an oblique stem in -īn-, e.g., Osc. dat. sg. **leginei**, acc. sg. **leginum**, *tanginom*, Umbr. abl. sg. **natine**. These would seem to correspond to the verbal abstract type of Latin *capiō, capiōnis* 'taking'. This inflection with -ō- throughout cannot be inherited in this category, and the contrast between the Latin and the Oscan and Umbrian paradigms suggests that Latin has regularized an inherited Italic alternation of -iō/-īn- by extending the -ō of the nominative throughout the paradigm.³ The Osco-Umbrian -īn- could conceivably go back to a sequence of either *-i̯i̯ŏ- or *-i̯i̯ĕ-. If we compare other *n*-stems, beside the type of Latin *sermō, sermōnis*, where the nom. sg. -ō has also been generalized, we find also the type of *homō, hominis*. The -ĭ- in the medial syllable of *hominis* could theoretically be the regular reduction of any short vowel, but the diminutive *homullus*, rather than *homellus*, should be from *-on-elo-. Therefore, it seems more likely that -īn- is the reflex of *-i̯i̯ŏ- and this development, too, can be dated to the Italic period.⁴

The treatment of the sequence *-i̯i̯ă- is even more difficult to illustrate, but there seems to be one likely example. The Latin for 'flute-player' is apparently an agent compound *tībīcen* < *tībii̯ă-kan-, which would seem to show that *-i̯i̯ă- developed regularly to -ī- also.

Finally, even *-i̯i̯ŭ- could have given the same result. Lat. *bīgae* 'two animals yoked together' is from *du̯i-i̯ŭg-, a compound of *du̯i- 'two' (> Lat. *bi-*) and the zero-grade of *i̯eug- 'join' (cf. *iugum* 'yoke', *iungō* 'join'). If this compound is of Italic date, the -ī- of *bīgae* would show that *-i̯i̯ŭ- was treated in the same way as the other sequences of *-i̯i̯V̆-.

If, therefore, as seems probable from the evidence above, the development of *-i̯i̯V̆- to -ī- in open syllables was accomplished within Italic, the *filie*-type of vocative is not an archaism, but rather an innovation that did not survive into the classical language.

NOTES

1. Cf. *O genitor noster Saturnie, maxime divum*, attributed to Ennius by Priscian (*ap. G. L.*, III.205.20 K). However, Ennius also has -ī in *Tatī* (*Ann.* 109 W).
2. Plautus' *Bromie* may well be simply modeled on the Greek form Βρόμιε (Ar. *Th.* 991).
3. The Oscan nominative of the type **úittiuf** (< *oi̯tiō+n+s) has had the -n- of the stem readded, plus an additional -s extended from the nominative singular of other stem types.
4. On the phonology of Italic *-i̯i̯o-, see now P. Schrijver, *MSS* 51 (1990), p. 243 ff.

10
Morta

Od. 10 W: '*quando dies adveniet quem profata Morta est*

Gellius[1] preserves this fragment as part of a discussion of the Fates (*Fatis tribus*, 3.16.9) and he understands the name *Morta* as equivalent to *Moera* 'Fate'. There seems to be no reason to doubt his statement. The use of the verb *profata est*, with its suggestion of *fatum* 'fate', would appear to confirm such an interpretation. Furthermore, modern scholars[2] usually associate the fragment with one or both of the Homeric passages:

εἰς ὅτε κέν μιν

μοῖρ' ὀλοὴ καθέλῃσι τανηλεγέος θανάτοιο (*Od.* 2.99–100)

and

ὁππότε κεν δὴ

μοῖρ'ὀλοὴ καθέλῃσι τανηλεγέος θανάτοιο (*Od.* 3.237–8).

If this fragment is translating one or the other of these passages, then it seems clear that Morta is serving in the capacity of μοῖρα.

Broccia[3], on the other hand, equates *dies* ... *quem profata Morta est* with the Homeric expression μόρσιμον ἦμαρ and remarks that μόρσιμος always means 'destined' or 'subject to destiny, fate'.[4]

Whatever the precise Homeric expression being translated, it seems clear that Livius has chosen *Morta* to function as the goddess of fate, the equivalent of μοῖρα, and hence *Morta* should mean something like 'fate' as well. Less clear, however, are the etymology and morphology of the name, to which we shall now turn.

Both μοῖρα and μόρσιμος are from a root **(s)mer-*, which also forms in Greek the verbs μείρομαι 'get as one's share' (< **(s)mer-i̯e/o-*) and ἔμμορε 'have one's share' and the substantives μέρος, μερίς 'part, share, lot' and μόρος 'fate'. The root is represented in Latin as well, in the verb *mereo(r)*, which would appear to have essentially the same underlying meaning as μείρομαι, but certainly a different morphological structure.

The surface -*ē*- of the present stem *merē*- could have resulted, in principle, from more than one source. Many verbs eventually have a stem in -*ē*- as the result

7

of a contraction of a suffix *-é-i̯e/o-. Verbs with this inherited suffix are usually divided, on the basis of their semantics, into two categories: the causatives, e.g., monēre 'to cause to remember' (cf. meminī), and the iteratives, e.g., torquēre 'to twist'.[5]

As these examples illustrate, both causatives and iteratives typically show o-grade of the root, and so one might object to analyzing mereo(r) as a causative/iterative on the grounds of its root vocalism. But e-grade causatives and iteratives are not unknown in Latin. One such causative is vegēre 'to cause to be lively'. Among the iteratives, we find medērī 'to heal' from *med- 'measure', although the o-grade of this root is well attested in Latin modus, modestus, and moderāre.

Moreover, this e-vocalism of the root, at least in vegeō and mereo(r), cannot be a very recent replacement of an o-grade since their to-participles are attested as vegĕto- and merĕto-.[6] In both cases the -e- of the root has prevented the medial -ĕ- from undergoing the regular reduction of internal short vowels to -ĭ-.[7] Of course, in the case of merĕto-, vowel weakening does eventually prevail, giving the more familiar form merito-. Nevertheless, these forms in -ĕto- are evidence that the e-vocalism of vegeō and mereo(r) was already established before the time of the normal vowel reductions and, therefore, must be of considerable age.[8]

Hence, mereo(r) is morphologically compatible with the causatives and iteratives, but its meaning must be considered. Since mereo(r) cannot be interpreted as 'cause to apportion', it would be necessary to classify it with the iteratives, if the -ē- of its stem goes back to *-éi̯e/o-.

On the other hand, the -ē- of merē- may not be a contraction of *-éi̯e/o- at all. Another large component of the second conjugation are the characterized stative presents in -ē-, e.g., tacēre 'to be silent'. But if the stem merē- belongs rather to this class, its root vocalism is again somewhat unexpected. Typically statives are formed with the zero-grade of the root, where phonotactically feasible, as in lubēre and vidēre. Latin can, however, show a syllabic treatment of a zero-grade when a root ends in a resonant. For example, *men- 'remain' would make a monosyllabic stem of the shape *mn-ē-, but this becomes *mn̥n-ē-, whence manēre. Therefore, we might rather expect a root *(s)mer- to form a stative stem *marē- < *mr̥r-ē- ← *mr-ē-. But, as with the causative/iteratives, Latin does have a few statives with e-grade from roots of this shape, such as tenēre 'to hold' and verērī 'to be in awe, to be afraid'.

It would seem, therefore, that mereo(r) could be classified as either an iterative or a stative. But the fact that mereo(r) is essentially synonymous with Gk. μείρομαι suggests that the two verbs may be part of a known pattern of Latin and Baltic presents in stative -ē- that correspond to Greek and Indo-Iranian i̯e/o-presents with similar meanings, cf. Lat. manēnre beside Av. (fra) manyeinte and, probably, Lat.

horrēre beside Skt. *hṛṣyati*.⁹ The equation of *mereo(r)* and μείρομαι is fairly compelling evidence for analyzing *mereo(r)* as a stative rather than an iterative.

In either case, the expected participle *mr̥-to-, had it not been replaced by *merĕto-*, would have given *morto-* by regular phonological development. Semantically, the *to*-participle of *mereo(r)* should mean 'received as one's share'. The feminine, *mortā*, of this stem could have been substantivized in the meaning 'that which is received as one's share' and hence 'one's lot or fate'. This would provide a perfectly appropriate word to render μοῖρα and so *Morta* may preserve a trace of the original form of the participle of *mereo(r)*.

It is quite likely, however, that the name *Morta* would at the same time have conjured up for the Romans, as it does for many modern readers, the idea of death, *mors* (*morti-*). Mariotti,¹⁰ while not ruling out an etymological connection between *Morta* and *mors*, imagines that this association allowed Livius to capture in a single word the Homeric expression μοῖρ' ὀλοὴ ... θανάτοιο.

Although the semantic context of *Morta* would seem to require the root etymology discussed above, it is nevertheless true that the root **mer-* of *morior*, *mors*, etc. formed a primary *to*-participle **mr̥-to-* 'dead' (> Skt. *mr̥ta-*, Gk. (ἄ)μβροτος), which would also have given **morto-* in Latin, identical to the corresponding form of **(s)mer-* 'to get a share'. If Latin had an inherited **morto-* 'dead', *Morta* could, in theory, be a verbal abstract 'death' substantivized from this participle. Latin does have other examples of abstract nouns in *-ā-* from *to*-participles, e.g., *fossa* 'ditch' (*fodiō*), *secta* 'course followed, path' (*sequor*; from an obsolete participle replaced by *secūtus*).

Although there is every possibility that **mr̥-to-* survived into Italic, the synchronic *to*-participle of Lat. *morior* is not *mortus, but *mortuus*, a form whose origin has never been satisfactorily explained. A commonly held theory¹¹ sets up for *mortuus* a pre-form **mr̥-tu̯o-*, which is said to be the result of the contamination of two forms that Italic could have inherited, **mr̥-to-* and **mr̥-u̯o-* (> OIr. *marb*, W. *marw* 'dead'). Such a hybrid form is apparently paralleled by OCS *mrĭtvŭ* < **mr̥-tu̯o-*.

The difficulty with this theory lies in the assumption that an internal *-tu̯-* would have developed to *-tuu̯-* in Latin. Anaptyxis would seem to be out of the question; nowhere else in the language does an anaptyctic vowel develop before a *-u̯-*. On the contrary, there seems to be an opposite tendency to syncopate a short vowel before *-u̯-*, at least when the vowel is preceded by a resonant, e.g. *arvum* < **ara-u̯o-m*.¹²

The regular phonological development of *-tu̯-* is virtually impossible to determine due to the paucity of words that certainly contained this sequence. It has been suggested that *-tu̯-* > *-p-* in Latin, but the only evidence for this development of non-initial *-tu̯-* is an etymology that reconstructs *aperiō* 'uncover, open' as *at-u̯er-, identical in root and preverb to Lith. àt-veriu 'open'. If correct, this would contradict the idea that *mortuus* could be phonologically regular from *mr̥-tu̯o-, but the etymology is far from secure.[13]

One other place to reconstruct -*tu*- is in the paradigm of the inherited word for 'four', whose stem would have appeared as *kʷt-ur̥- before consonants and *kʷt-ur- before vowels. But Lat. *quattuor* shows a sequence -*ttu*- that does not directly continue either one of these. *Quattuor* may very well represent the result of combining the varying stems into a single, indeclinable form. The stem *kʷt-ur- could account for the syllabic -*u*-[14] and so it is tempting to think that the -*tt*- is the actual outcome of the -*tu̯*- of *kʷt-ur̥-. If it does not somehow continue -*tu̯*-, the -*tt*- of *quattuor* is extremely difficult to explain.

Therefore, it is almost impossible to accept that -*tu̯*- could have given -*tuu̯*- by any regular phonological process. Since the contamination approach is plagued with apparently irresolvable phonological problems, it seems worthwhile to re-analyze the morphology of *mortuus*. Latin has two major types of adjectives in -*uus* (-*uu̯o-*): the deverbative type, e.g., *occiduus* 'sinking, setting' (lit. 'falling down', cf. *cadō*) and *perspicuus* 'clear, transparent' (lit. 'seen through', cf. *speciō*),[15] and the denominative type, e.g., *fatuus* 'feeble(-minded)' from the *o*-stem adjective **fato-* 'tired', whose existence is implied by the substantive **fatis* (in *adfatim*).[16] The correspondence between **fato-* and *fatuus* raises the possibility that the inherited *to*-participle **mr̥-to-* may have had beside it a synonymous deadjectival *mortuus*.

How an adjective in -*uu̯o-* would have been created beside one in -*o-* is yet another question; some intermediate stage would seem to be necessary. Indo-European had a process by which a *u*-stem substantive could be derived from an *o*-stem adjective, for example from **ai̯sto-* 'hot' (> OE *āst* 'drying oven') was derived **ai̯stu-* 'heat' (> Lat. *aestus*). In fact a *tu*-stem verbal abstract **mr̥-tu-* 'death' is found in Arm. *mah* (older *marh*).[17] There are also parallels for the creation of *o*-stem adjectives from *u*-stem substantives. For example, in Greek we find ἀστός (< **u̯astu-ó-*) 'townsman' derived from ἄστυ 'town'. Therefore, it is possible that from the primary *to*-participle **mr̥-to-* 'dead' was derived a *u*-stem **mr̥-tu-*, from which in turn a new *o*-stem adjective, **mr̥tu-o-*, was formed. This is the form that was inherited into Italic and Slavic.

But, as discussed above, OCS *mrĭtvŭ* and Lat. *mortuus* differ in their immediate pre-forms. The two can be reconciled by assuming a difference in the syllabification of **mr̥-tu-o-*. OCS *mrĭtvŭ* is the result of syllabifying **mr̥tu-o-* as **mr̥tu̯-o-*. But in Latin, the syllabicity of the -*u*- was preserved by the insertion of the homorganic glide -*u̯*-, giving the pre-form **mr̥tuu̯-o-* (> *mortuus*).[18] Such an adjective derived from a *u*-stem was apparently synonymous with the original *o*-stem one from which it was indirectly derived and thus *mortuus* was able to completely replace the expected **morto-*.

Livius' naming of the goddess of fate as *Morta* may have been influenced by the surface similarity, and reasonably appropriate semantics, of *mortuus*, etc. But the fact that *Morta* is translating μοῖρα suggests that it is more likely to mean 'Fate' than 'Death' and to belong etymologically to the same family as *mereo(r)*, μείρομαι, and μοῖρα itself.

NOTES

1. 3.16.11: *Caesellius autem Vindex in Lectionibus suis Antiquis: "Tria," inquit, "nomina Parcarum sunt: 'Nona,' 'Decuma,' 'Morta,'" et versum hunc Livii, antiquissimi poetae, ponit ex* 'Οδυσσεία... *Sed homo minime malus Caesellius "Mortam" quasi nomen accepit, cum accipere quasi Moeram deberat.*
2. Mariotti (p. 95) and Verrusio (*Livio Andronico e la sua traduzione dell' Odissea omerica* [Rome, 1977], p. 45 f.), among others.
3. *Recerche su Livio Andronico Epico* (Padua, 1974), p. 57.
4. μόρσιμος is thus synonymous with αἴσιμος (cf. αἴσιμον ἦμαρ, π 280, Θ 72, Χ 212) and has probably been remade from μόριμος (Υ 302) under the influence of αἴσιμος.
5. Although it is useful to speak of two semantic categories, the two do share this common morphology and may ultimately go back to a single class in the proto-language.
6. *Vegeto-* is found throughout classical Latin and the form *mereto-* is attested in inscriptions as late as 130–90 BC (*CIL* 1.2.1529).
7. The non-weakening of a short vowel in a medial syllable due to the influence of a like vowel in the preceding, initial syllable is commonly known as the *alacer*-rule.
8. Not even *merĕto-* can have been the original *to*-participle of *mereo(r)*, though, which should have been formed by adding the suffix *-to-* directly to the zero-grade of the root, giving a pre-form *$m\rline{r}$-to-* from the root *mer-*. The participles in *-ĕto-* of the causatives/iteratives are rather analogical to the *to*-participles of verbs of the *capiō*-type by the proportion *kapi̯e/o-* : *kapto-* : : *merei̯e/o-* : X = *merĕto-*.
9. See Schmid, p. 67.
10. Marrioti, p. 37, n. 1.
11. See W-H and Sihler (§ 185.4.a), among others. Bréal (*MSL* 6 [1889], p. 127) also proposes a contamination, but of *morto-* directly with its opposite *vīvo-* 'alive'.
12. For syncope before *-u̯-*, see further the section on *pullus*.
13. See, for example, the discussion of *aperiō* in E-M.
14. The generalization of the *u*-vowel in the word for 'four' is paralleled by Hom. πίσυρες.
15. On this type see also the Appendix.
16. The derivation of *i*-stem substantives from *o*-stem adjectives was an IE process; compare *$h_2e\hat{k}$-ro-* (> Gk. ἄκρος) → *$h_2e\hat{k}$-ri-* (> Gk. ἄκρις and perhaps Skt. *áśri-*, unless this goes back to *$h_2o\hat{k}$-ri-*, with Gk. ὄκρις and Lat. *ocris*).
17. See Pokorny, 4. *mer-*.
18. This sort of variety in syllabification is paralleled elsewhere in IE. Within Greek, the sequence *pedi-o-* (an *o*-stem derivative of the old locative of 'foot') is treated as both *pedi̯o-* (> πεζός) and *pedii̯o-* (> πεδίον).

15
nequīnont
36
inserinuntur

Od. 15 W: *partim errant, nequinont Graecam redire;*
Od. 34–36 W: *Topper citi ad aedis venimus Circai;*
           simul † duona † carnem portant ad navis
           multam ancillae; vina isdem inserinuntur.

Livius preserves two members, *nequīnont* and *inserinuntur*, of an unusual set of verbal forms with a third plural present ending *-nont(ur)* or the regular development thereof, *-nunt(ur)*. The rest of the set consists of *danunt* (= *dant*), *explēnunt* (= *explent*), *solinunt* (= *solent*), *ferīnunt* (= *feriunt*), and *obīnunt*, *prodīnunt*, and *redīnunt* (= *-eunt*). Of these, *danunt* is the only one attested more than once; it occurs twelve or thirteen times in Plautus, once each in Caecilius, Naevius, and Pacuvius, and in *CIL* 1.2.1531.[1] *Prodīnunt* and *redīnunt* are found in Ennius.[2] The other forms, with the glosses given above, are only cited by Festus,[3] who also is the source of these Livian and Ennian fragments. The long *-ī-* in the compounds of *eō* is therefore metrically guaranteed,[4] as is the short *-ă-* of *danunt*. The quantities indicated for the other forms will be justified by an explanation of their origin that will be presented shortly.

Several theories of the origin of the *-nunt* have been advanced, although none seems to have won anything like universal acceptance. One of the most popular ideas takes the *eō* compounds as the first bearers of the ending and connects the extra *-n-* with that of Lith. *einù* 'go' and/or Hitt. *iyannai-* 'start moving'.[5] But in those verbs the *-n-* recurs throughout their paradigms, whereas in Latin it is confined to the third plural.[6] It is quite implausible that this distribution in Latin is coincidental.

Other scholars have taken *danunt* as the starting point for the ending, apparently on the grounds that it is the only such form attested with any frequency. Pedersen[7] and Johansson[8] proposed very similar scenarios, both assuming the loss of the final consonant from *dant* giving a *dan to which the ending *-unt* was added in order to give the form more of the appearance of a third plural. This loss of final *-t* is a common development only in vulgar Latin and the very few archaic examples (e.g., **dedron** '*dederunt*', *CIL* 1.2.30) appear in inscriptions that are generally agreed to show non-Roman dialect features.[9] Although this hypothesis takes into account the distributional facts, it nevertheless seems improbable, since one would have to believe that of all the third plurals in *-nt*, only *dant* lost its final consonant at such an early date.

13

Pierri's suggestion of a cross between *dōnant* and *dant* simply does not work.[10] Clearly, neither *dōnant* nor *dant* can have supplied the *-unt* of *danunt*.

Vine, following Walde,[11] proposed that a form **danṇt* (> *danunt*) was introduced as a disyllabic replacement of *dant* under the pressure of the disyllabic first and second plural forms, *damus* and *datis*. Aside from the phonological difficulty of getting *danunt* from a preform **danṇt*, the motivation for such a replacement is questionable. As Otrębski notes, Latin consistently shows the pattern of a third plural form one syllable shorter than the corresponding first and second plurals, as in *-āmus, -ātis, -ant; -ēmus, -ētis, -ent*; and *-imus, -itis, -unt*.[12] This holds true for the active infectum forms, indicative and subjunctive, of every regular conjugation, except the present active indicative of stems in **-(i)i̯e/o-*, that is, the types of *capiō* and *audiō*. In fact, there seems rather to have been pressure to enforce the *-āmus, -ātis, -ant* type of pattern, to judge from the present subjunctive paradigm of the verb 'to be', in which the older *sīmus, sītis, sient* (all disyllabic) was remade to *sīmus, sītis, sint*. Thus *damus* and *datis* are unlikely to have influenced *dant* to match their syllable count; on the contrary, they may have played a role in preventing *danunt* from gaining widespread popularity. This tendency for the third person plural to be one syllable shorter than the first and second makes a reformation of *dant* to **danṇt* seem unlikely. Furthermore, there are no parallels for even a secondary syllabic **-ṇ-* giving *-un-* in Latin.

Sommer, also supposing *danunt* to be the prototype of the group, proposed that it was created analogically according to the proportion, *sĭtus : sinunt :: dătus : X = danunt*.[13] Also, *sinō* is not the only verb with a third plural of the surface structure *X-n-unt* beside a *to*-participle in *X-to-*; there are *linunt : lĭtus* and *cernunt : certus*.[14] This analogy is formally unobjectionable, but leaves open the question of why any of these verbs should have had an influence on *dō* and then only on the third plural.

To answer the first of these questions, some point of contact, other than the *to*-participle, is needed between *dō* and one or more of the verbs *sinō, linō*, and *cernō*. Such a connection can be identified for *dō* and *sinō*; the two verbs overlap semantically to some extent. The range of meanings for each includes 'grant, allow'. This is the usual meaning of *sinō*; an example of this usage of *dō* can be found at Pl. *Am.* 11:

> nam vos quidem id iam scitis concessum et datum
> mi esse ab dis aliis, nuntiis praesim et lucro–.

This semantic similarity provides the required point of contact between *danunt* and its proposed analogical model *sinunt*.

The final question that must be asked in connection with Sommer's theory is, what would have been the motivation for the creation of *danunt*? *Dant* was obviously not intolerable, but it is undoubtedly very short and a more substantial form may have been desirable. There is reason to believe that the length of a word was sometimes a consideration in Latin. For example, the imperative singular of *sciō* is always *scītō*, not **scī*. Moreover, the most common *-nunt* forms after *danunt*, namely the *-īnunt* (= *-eunt*) forms, are also associated with an exceptionally short present stem. In this connection it may also be relevant to mention the fact that the simplex forms of *pleō* are fairly infrequent, at least compared to its compounds, and that the third plural **plent* does not seem to be attested at all. The motivating factor, therefore, seems not to have been the fact that *dant* was one syllable shorter than *damus* and *datis*, but that *dant* was just one syllable in all.

Furthermore, with the exception of a single inscription, none of the *-nunt* forms is attested outside of the more archaic poets, if the context is known at all. This would seem to suggest that metrical considerations may have played some role. All of the occurrences of *danunt* in Plautus are in iambic and trochaic meters, eight of the twelve[15] occur at the end of the line, where such a metrical structure would be most convenient. Also, the metrical structure of *nequīnont* (˘ ‒ ‒) seems to have been decidedly preferable to that of *neqeunt* (˘ ˘ ‒) for a trisyllabic word in this position in a Saturnian line.[16]

The analogy *sītus* : *sinunt* : : *dătus* : X = *danunt*, proposed by Sommer, provides the most convincing explanation of the origin of *danunt*. Once *danunt* had been analogically created, the other *-nunt* forms were very probably modeled on it. Although the *to*-participles may have again served as the point of contact in the cases of *explēnunt* (: *explētus*), *solīnunt* (: *solītus*) and *ferīnunt* (: *ferītus*), this will not work for the *eō* compounds, including *nequeō*, or *inserinuntur*; by that analogy the forms would have come out **-īnunt* (: *-ītus*) and **insernuntur* (: *insertus*). How, then, are we to account for these forms?

Danunt, *explēnunt*, *solīnunt*, and *ferīnunt* are undoubtedly present tense forms and, once established as variants of *dant*, etc., there would have been no particular reason to continue to associate them exclusively with the *to*-participles. The paradigms *damus*, *datis*, *danunt*, *explēmus*, *explētis*, *explēnunt*, and *ferīmus*, *ferītis*, *ferīnunt* could easily have prompted a different analogy, so that *-īnunt* was created beside *-īmus*, *-ītis* and *inserīnuntur* beside *inserimus*, *inseritis*.

The analogy does not seem to have affected the paradigm of these verbs beyond the third plural, with one possible exception. Festus preserves a form *solinō*, for which he reports the gloss '*consulō*'.[17] If this meaning is correct, *solinō* cannot be from the same paradigm as *solinunt*, which Festus glosses '*solent*'.[18] If, however, the definition '*consulō*' is simply an error, *solinō* may show that the analogy did begin to proceed a bit further, but apparently did not get far before these forms fell into disuse.

To summarize, the third plurals in *-nunt* are all modeled, by one analogy or another, on the form *danunt*, which is itself an analogical variant of *dant* created by the Sommer's proportion *sītus* : *sinunt* : : *dătus* : X = *danunt*. The semantic overlap between the two verbs explains why the paradigm of *sinō* could have influenced that of *dō*, although Sommer does not make this explicit. This scenario describes how *danunt* was created, but not why. The preference of *danunt* for line-end position in iambic and trochaic verse suggests that its appearance was metrically conditioned; the other *-nunt* forms, as far as can be determined, are found almost exclusively in poetry. Another factor seems to have been that *dant* was a monosyllabic verbal form—something not highly desirable to judge from, for example, the use of *scītō* for **scī*. On the other hand, *danunt* did not survive into the classical language. This was probably due to the tendency of third plural present forms to be one syllable shorter than the corresponding first and second plural forms, a pattern whose influence can be observed in the replacement of *sient* by *sint*. This pressure seems to have reinforced the pattern of *damus, datis, dant*, and caused the eventual disappearance of the innovated *-nunt* forms.

NOTES

1. Caecil. *fab.* 170 W: *Patiere quod dant, quando optata non danunt.* Naev. B. P. 36 W: *eam carnem victoribus danunt.* Pac. tr. 218–219 W: *Di me etsi perdunt, tamen esse adiutam expetunt | quom prius quam intereo spatium ulciscendi danunt.* Pl. Capt. 819, Curc. 126 (*dant*, cdd.), Merc. 226, Most. 129, 561, Pers. 256, 852, Poen. 1253, Pseud. 767, 770, Rud. 594, Truc. 181, 245.
2. Ann. 158 W: *Prodinunt famuli: tum candida lumina lucent. Redīnunt* is attributed to Ennius by Festus, but the line is not preserved (p. 287 M).
3. *explēnunt*, p. 80 M; *ferīnunt, solinunt*, p. 162 M; *obīnunt*, p. 189 M.
4. It is clear that the Romans considered *nequeō*, whatever its ultimate history, to be a compound of *eō*, whose inflection it follows. It will be assumed to pattern with the other *eō* compounds in the following discussion.
5. In favor of a Lithuanian connection are Krause (*KZ* 69, p. 163) and Otrębski (*Eos* 33, p. 325–331).
6. The one possible exception, *solinō*, will be discussed below.
7. *IF* 2, p. 302
8. *Akadem. afhandl. til S. Burge*, p. 30 f.
9. Although *CIL* 1.2.30 is from Rome, **dedron** has the syncope (or syllabic notation) characteristic of Oscan- and Umbrian-speaking regions, cf. **dedro** '*dederunt*' (*CIL* 1.2.379) from Pisaurum. See Vine, p. 339.
10. *Riv. Fil.* 33, p. 496.
11. Vine, p. 203; Walde, *WklPh.* 1915, p. 793.
12. cf. also *sumus, estis, sunt*.
13. *Kritische Erläuterungen*, p. 192.
14. *Certus* (< **kri-to-*, cf. Gk. κριτός) was the original *to*-participle of *cernō* (< **krin-$^e/_o$-*, cf. Gk. κρίνω).
15. Or nine of thirteen, if one accepts the emendation of *potantes danunt* for *potantes dant* at *Curc.* 126.
16. A detailed discussion of the preferred scansion of trisyllabic words after the *caesura Korschiana* can be found in the comment on *dextrābus* below.
17. p. 351 M; the definition is attributed to Messala augur.
18. See above, note 3.

25, 33, 34
topper

Od. 23–26 W: ... *namque nullum*
                         peius macerat humanum quamde mare saevum;
                         vires cui sunt magnae topper confringent
                         importunae undae.
Od. 33 W: *Topper facit homones ut prius fuerunt,*
Od. 34–36 W: *Topper citi ad aedis venimus Circai*
                 simul † duona † carnem portant ad navis,
                 multam ancillae; vina isdem inserinuntur.

    The adverb *topper* is attested in context only in the fragments of the more archaic writers. Beside the three examples in Livius above, it occurs once each in

Naevius:

        Topper capesset flammam Volcani. (B. P. 50 W),

Ennius:

        Topper quam nemo melius scit (*Inc.* 437 W),

Accius:

        Topper, ut fit, patris te eicit ira. (*Tr.* 380 W),

Pacuvius:

        Topper tecum, sist potestas, faxsit; sin mecum velit, (*Inc.* 29 W),

the *Carmen Nelei*:

        Topper fortunae commutantur hominibus. (fr. 5 W),

and Coelius Antipater:

        Ita uti sese quisque vobis studeat aemulari in statu fortunae rei publicae, eadem re gesta, topper nihilo minore negotio acto, gratia minor esset.

                                                           (47.1 ff.).[1]

These fragments are all preserved in Festus (p. 352 M) as illustrations of the definitions of *topper* given by Artorius (*cito, fortasse, celeriter, temere* 'quickly, perhaps, swiftly, rashly') and Sinnius (*Topper fortasse valet in Enni et Pacui scriptis ... at in antiquissimis scriptis celeriter ac mature.* '*Topper* means "perhaps" in the writings of Ennius and Pacuvius, but in the most ancient writings "swiftly" and "seasonably" '). The passages of Livius, Naevius, and the *Carmen Nelei* are quoted to exemplify *topper* in the sense of 'quickly', whereas the others are said to show *topper* meaning 'perhaps'.

The word is clearly archaic and seems to have fallen into disuse by the Classical period,[2] so that even its meaning eventually became unclear. Neither of the basic meanings 'quickly' or 'perhaps' suits all the instances of *topper*. Also, it seems possible that the grammarians tried to infer the sense of the obsolete word from context. The meaning 'quickly' may well have been suggested by Livius' "*Topper citi ...* ". But the very fact that *topper* is followed immediately by *citi* argues against the two words being synonymous. 'Perhaps' may simply have been vague enough to cover any case where 'quickly' was definitely inappropriate. If, on the other hand, the definitions recorded in Festus are essentially correct, it is not very easy to see how one could be a semantic development of the other, or what earlier meaning could have undergone such a semantic split as to yield both. Since we should not, therefore, have complete faith in the statements of the grammarians, it may be profitable to use other methods to determine independently, if possible, the sense of *topper*.

One obvious way to begin is to examine the context of the word, but this method cannot be expected to reveal much more to modern scholars than it did to the ancients. The context fails not only to confirm the translations quoted in Festus, but also to suggest any reasonably sure alternative. It may prove useful to note, however, that in seven of the nine passages, *topper* is the initial word of the sentence. Although word order is an admittedly unstable basis for argument, this decided preference for sentence-initial position seems, nevertheless, to be most consistent with a conjunction or adverb indicating how the sentence introduced by *topper* is connected to what precedes it. Unfortunately, the fragmentary nature of the evidence makes it very difficult to tell what sort of connection might be indicated.

If context alone cannot provide a meaning for *topper*, perhaps its etymology may offer a clue. Simply by inspection, *topper* is probably to be classed with a group of Latin adverbs made with a suffix *-per*. The other members are:

nūper 'newly, recently, just now' (Pl. +)
semper 'always, ever, regularly' (Pl. +)
parumper 'for/in a short time' (Enn. +)
paul(l)umper 'for a short time' (*CIL* 8.9642)
paul(l)isper 'for a short time' (Pl. +)

pauxillisper 'by slow degrees, bit by bit' (Pl.+)
aliquantisper 'for some time' (Pl.+)
quantisper 'for how long a time?' (Caecil.+)
tantisper 'for such time'; 'for the meantime' (Pl.+)

Of these *parumper* and *paul(l)umper* can be understood synchronically as *parum* and *paul(l)um*, both meaning '(a) little', plus *-per*. In this formation, *parum* and *paul(l)um* are almost certainly the neuter accusative singulars of the adjectives,[3] the accusative being the case used to indicate duration of time.

Semper also contains a neuter accusative form, that of the inherited word for 'one', cf. Gk. ἕν < **sem*. But unlike *parum* and *paul(l)um*, **sem* has not been an independent element in Latin for some time and so *semper* must be of considerable age. Furthermore, *semper* certainly appears to be of the same formation as Umbr. **triiu-per** 'thrice' and Osc. *pertiro-pert* 'four times', in which a suffix *-per(t)* is joined postpositively to the neuter accusative of the numerals.[4] Therefore, at an earlier time, *semper* should have meant 'once'. The transition from 'once' to 'always, forever' is of some interest. One could imagine 'forever' as a single period of time extended indefinitely, but it seems impossible to trace the route of the development within attested Latin. Such a semantic development is not improbable, however, since a parallel one seems to have taken place in Germanic, where Go. *sim(b)lē* means 'once, formerly', but OHG *simble(s)*, *simblom* and OE *sim(b)le(s)* mean 'always'.[5] These adverbs undoubtedly contain this **sem* plus some suffixal material reminiscent of Lat. *semel* 'once' and *simul* 'at one and the same time'.[6] A mid-stage in the Germanic semantic evolution is likely to have been a sense of 'once and for all', which is also one of the possible translations of *semel*.[7] The semantics of *semper* may well have followed a similar course.

The forms in *-isper*, however, clearly do not contain neuter accusative forms, either singular or plural, of the adjectives. Nor could the non-neuter *o*-stem or *ā*-stem accusative plurals be the basis of *-isper*. If the *-i-* is long, which seems to be the standard opinion,[8] the *-isper* adverbs could be made from masculine or feminine *i*-stem substantivizations of the *o*-stem adjectives of the type *rāvis* 'hoarseness' to *rāvus* 'hoarse'. While this presents no phonological difficulties, two objections can be raised. First, there is no other trace of the *i*-stem substantives **tantis*, **paul(l)is*, etc. Second, Latin already has substantives from *tantus* and *paul(l)us*, for example, namely the substantivized neuter singular forms *tantum* and *paul(l)um*. This, in turn, raises the question of what purpose a plural would have served in most of the attested Latin examples. Semantically, there is no need for one: *paul(l)isper* means the same as *paul(l)umper*, 'for a short time'.

Of the other *-isper* adverbs, *aliquantisper*, *quantisper*, and *tantisper* also refer to a duration of time. This sense, 'for X amount of time', would seem to have become the default meaning for all relatively new *-per* adverbs. The one non-conformist is *pauxillisper*, defined by the *OLD* as 'by slow degrees, bit by bit' and attested from Plautus onward. The fact that this does not correspond to the durative sense of the productive formation implies that *pauxillisper* is preserving a more archaic meaning. The adjective *pauxillus* means '(very) little' and so *pauxillisper* can be understood as 'by little bits', which would explain the apparent use of a plural form.

As for the case of the form, a non-neuter accusative plural seems very unlikely. Firstly, it is hard to imagine why the neuter plural would not have been used, as in the Oscan and Umbrian parallels, if a plural form was required. Secondly, it is not clear how an accusative form, even of another gender, could be the basis of an adverb meaning 'by little bits'. The meaning of *pauxillisper* is more reminiscent of the instrumental use of the ablative, as in *paul(l)ō* 'by a little'.[9] The plural equivalent of this would give just the right sense for *pauxillisper*. Thus it is more likely that the *-īs-* is the ending of the ablative plural. Nevertheless, the distinction in meaning between adverbs made from accusative plus *-per* and ablative plus *-per* seems to have become blurred fairly early in the history of Latin, since all the *-isper* adverbs except *pauxillisper* have the durative sense proper to the accusative-based type, even though they are all attested from the time of Plautus or Caecilius. Why this distinction was lost remains an open question.

One *-per* adverb, *nūper*, cannot be connected with a case-form at all. Like **sem*, the **nū* of *nūper* is no longer a free-standing word in Latin, but is inherited, cf. Skt. *nū* and Gk. νῦν. Sanskrit and Greek also preserve alternate forms with a short vowel, *nu* and νύ. But it is impossible to determine whether or not Latin inherited both the long and short forms because the only possible traces of the short form are ambiguous. *Nunc* 'now' would scan as long, even if the inherited quantity of the **-u-* were short. In any case, an inherited **-ū-* in **nūn-ce* would almost certainly have been shortened by Osthoff's Law.[10] Otherwise **nu* only appears in the univerbation *nudius* which is always followed by, and often written as a single word with, *tertius* (*quartus*, etc.). Although the first syllable is marked as short in Lewis and Short, the *OLD* leaves it unmarked, and there does indeed seem to be no way of guaranteeing the quantity. *Nudius*, followed by an ordinal, occurs nine times in Plautus in iambic or trochaic verses. Therefore, it is equally possible that we are dealing with an etymological *nŭdius tertius*, for example, scanned *nŭdĭus tértius*, or an etymological *nūdius tertius* scanned *nūdĭus tértius*, with iambic shortening.

There seems to be no doubt that *topper* is also formed with the same suffix *-per*, although to what the suffix has been added is not immediately apparent. One theory, however, has gained extremely widespread acceptance, namely that *topper* is the result of an assimilation of **tod-per*, in which **tod* is identified with the neuter accusative singular of the pronominal stem **to-*.[11] Therefore, we would again be dealing with quite an old formation, since **tod*, although inherited, is not attested as an independent word in Latin. If this is the correct etymology of *topper*, one must still ask how a demonstrative stem meaning 'this, that' could have come to mean 'quickly' and/or 'perhaps' by the simple addition of the *-per* suffix.

The only other trace of *tod in Latin is in the neuter pronoun *istud*, but other forms from the simple stem do still exist in Latin. The adverbs *tum* 'at that time, then' and *tam* 'to that extent, so' are its accusative singular masculine and feminine, respectively.[12] Given that *-per* makes temporal adverbs, *topper* might be expected to mean 'at that time, then'. This may very well have come to mean 'just then',[13] which makes perfect sense in all the passages where the ancient grammarians translate 'quickly', *vel sim*. The sense of immediacy conveyed by 'just then' could easily have created the impression that *topper* meant 'quickly'.[14]

On the other hand, the fragments of Pacuvius, Ennius, Coelius, and perhaps Accius seem to show a slightly different development of 'then', rather along the lines of English 'then' in the sense of 'in that case, accordingly'. Thus the Pacuvius fragment—*Topper tecum, sist potestas, faxsit; sin mecum velit*—could be translated, "Then let him do it with you, if he can, but if he wants to with me...."

Such an interpretation would confirm the earlier proposition that *topper*, with its tendency to be first in its sentence, should serve as a link to the sentence before. The connection could be strictly temporal, marking an event subsequent in time, or more consequential, indicating a circumstance that follows logically from what precedes. Above all, reconstructing a basic meaning 'then' for *topper* allows us to reconcile the apparent differences in meaning observed by the grammarians.

NOTES

1. Peter, *Historicorum Romanorum Fragmenta*.
2. Quintilian advises against the use of *topper* and other archaic words: ... *nihil est odiosius adfectatione, nec utique ab ultimis et iam oblitteratis repetita temporibus, qualia sunt topper et antegerio et exanclare et prosapia et Saliorum carmina vix sacerdotibus suis satis intellecta*. (1.6.40). See also Lebek, p. 36–9.
3. Although *parum* exists as an indeclinable noun, historically it is the old neut. nom.-acc. sg. of the adjective which became *parvus, -a, -um*. **Par-u̯o-m* became *parom by regular sound change and this gave *parum*, which was able to be retained as the noun/adverb because it had become dissociated from the adjectival paradigm, where the loss of *-*u̯*- before *-*o*- left a stem alternating between *par- and **paru̯*-. The paradigm was levelled in favor of **paru̯*-.
4. Buck *OU*, §192.2.
5. Something comparable also seems to be going on in modern English, where 'once' and 'ever' can be used interchangably in some circumstances. Consider, for example, "If once we lose heart, all is lost." and "In all his years at the nuclear plant, Homer didn't once remember to wear his radiation shield." In both these sorts of sentences, 'ever' can replace 'once', and yet 'ever' can, of course, mean 'always', as in 'evergreen'. Compare also such English expressions as "once broken, never mended".

6. Feist, p. 231.
7. *OLD* mg. 3.
8. The *-i-* is marked long in L-H, W-H, and Bader, for example.
9. *Paul(l)ō* itself appears most often with expressions of time (*prius, ante, post*, etc.) and with comparatives.
10. Cf. *ŭndecim*, for which the quantity of the initial vowel is shown by the Romance reflexes, e.g., Fr. *onze*. This episode of Osthoff must have been rather late, since it followed the change of *-*oi̯*- to -*ū*- and the syncope of the internal short vowel.
11. This idea is at least as early as Vaniček (1874) and is taken up by Brugmann (*Die Demonstrativpronomina der Indogermanischen Sprachen* [Leipzig, 1904]), W-H, E-M, L-H, etc.
12. Also *tunc* 'then' is from *tum-ce and *tandem* 'at last' from *tam-dem.
13. Cf. W-H, who translate *topper* "*gerade dann*". This is also rather like the common translation of *nūper* as 'just now'.
14. If *topper* had, at a sufficiently early stage, come to mean something closer to 'quickly', then it is not impossible that a meaning 'perhaps' could have developed from this. Greek offers a parallel in τάχα, which is clearly from the root of ταχύς, but can mean both 'quickly' and 'perhaps'. An example of the latter meaning is Hesiod's δίς μὲν γὰρ καὶ τρὶς τάχα τεύξεαι (*Op.* 401).

30
Monētās

Od. 30 W: '*nam divina Monetas filia docuit*

Priscian (*ap. G. L.*, II.198) cites this passage because *Monētās* shows the archaic *ā*-stem genitive singular ending, which is fairly well-attested in Old Latin, occurring twice more in Livius (*Lātōnās, escās*),[1] twice in Naevius (*fortūnās, terrās*),[2] and once in Ennius (*viās*),[3] and is preserved in Classical Latin in the adverb *aliās* and in the fixed, often univerbated, expressions *pater (filius*, etc.) *familiās*. This seems to have been the inherited Italic ending, as it is the only one attested in Oscan and Umbrian (e.g., Osc. *eituas* '*pecūniae*', Umbr. **tutas** '*cīvitātis*').

Monēta, also a cult-name for Juno,[4] is Livius' name for the mother of the Muses, his rendering of the Greek Μνημοσύνη "Memory". Μνημοσύνη is from the root **men(h₂)-* 'to think' and its connection to Greek verbs from this root must have been apparent. Therefore, it is not unreasonable to suspect that a name derived from a Latin verb from this very root would have been used by Livius as the Latin equivalent of Μνημοσύνη. One such verb is *moneō*, historically a causative going back to **mon-éi̯e/o*, with the characteristic root *o*-grade and causative suffix.[5] Although one might object that *moneō* could no longer be synchronically recognized as akin to words having to do with remembering, there is some evidence that the Romans still believed the verb to be related to these known cognates. Varro says that *meminisse* is from *memoria* and that *monēre* is from this same word.[6] Of course, the relationship between these words is not derivational in the way Varro describes, nor is *memoria* even from the same root as the two verbs,[7] but the fact remains that a connection is recognized.

The surface similarity of *moneō* to *Monēta* caused ancient scholars to suppose that the two were related. Cicero tells the story of how Juno got the title *Monēta* and he uses *moneō* to describe her action on that occasion.[8] But what process could have produced such a derivative from this verb?

Latin does have a set of nouns characterized by a suffix-like element **-ēto-*, which has become fairly productive, usually to designate a place where a certain sort of plant-life grows, as in *cupressētum* 'cypress-wood' from *cypressus*. At this point it will be useful to examine the history of this nominal type in Latin, beginning with an inventory organized semantically.[9]

Places where trees grow:

aesculētum 'a forest of *aesculus*' (Var.+)
arborētum 'a plantation of trees' (Quad.+)

23

buxētum 'a boxwood-plantation' (Mart.)
castan(i)ētum 'a chestnut-plantation' (Col.+)
cornētum 'a plantation of cornel-trees' (Var.)
corylētum 'a hazel-thicket' (Ov.)
cupressētum 'a cypress-wood' (Cato+)
ficētum 'a fig-orchard' (Var.+)
īlicētum 'a grove of holm-oaks' (Mart.+)
mālētum 'an orchard' (Suet.)
myrtēta 'a myrtle grove' (Pl.)[10]
myrtētum (*mur-*) 'a myrtle grove' (Pl.+)
nucētum 'a nut-grove' (Stat.)
olētum 'an olive-yard' (Cato)
olīvētum 'an olive-yard' (Cato+)[11]
palmētum 'a palm-grove' (Hor.+)
pīnētum 'a pine-wood' (Prop.+)
pōmētum 'an orchard' (Suet.)
pōpulētum 'a plantation of poplar-trees' (Plin.)
querquētum (*querc-*) 'an oak-wood' (Var.+)
rumpotinētum 'a plantation of dwarf trees' (Col.)
salictētum 'an osier-bed' (Ulp.)[12]

Places where other plants grow:

dūmētum 'a clump of thorn, bushes, thicket' (Cic+)
fruticētum 'a thicket of shrubs or bushes' (Hor.+)
(h)arundinētum 'a reed-bed' (Cato+)
iuncētum 'a place where rushes grow, bed of rushes' (Var.)
rosētum 'a rose-garden' (Verg.)
rubētum 'a thicket of brambles' (Ov.+)
senticētum 'a place full of thorns or brambles, thicket' (Pl.+)
spīnētum 'a thicket of thorns' (Verg.+)
vīminētum 'a place where withies are cut, osier-bed' (Var.)
vīnētum 'a plantation of vines, vineyard' (Var.+)
virgētum 'a place full of brushwood or withies' (Cic.)

Places where types of stones are found:

sabulētum 'a gravel-pit' (Plin.)
saxētum 'a stone-quarry' (Cic.+)
sepulcrētum 'a graveyard' (Catul.)[13]

Places where things other than flora or stones are found:

būcētum 'a pasture for cattle' (Var.+)[14]
porculētum 'a "ridged" field' (Plin.)[15]

Other sorts of places:

asprētum 'a piece of rough ground' (Liv.+)
veterētum 'a piece of ground that has stood fallow for some time' (Col.)

A collection of the produce of a plant:

olīvēta 'an olive-harvest' (Fest.)

Vines or parts thereof:

fūnētum 'a vine trained so as to form an arbor' (Plin.)[16]
masculētum 'a male or sterile growth (on a vine)' (Plin.)

Things that smell bad:

fimētum 'a dung-heap' (Plin.)
olenticētum 'a foul-smelling place' (Apul.)
olētum 'excrement' (Veran. *ap.* Paul. *Fest.*+)

Comestible fluids:

acētum 'vinegar' (Pl.+)
tēmētum 'any intoxicating liquor, strong drink' (Pl.+)

Culinary dishes:[17]

cocētum 'a kind of food made from honey and poppies' (Paul. *Fest.*+)[18]
morētum 'a dish made with cheese and pounded herbs' (*Mor.*+)[19]
tuccētum 'some made-up savory dish' (Pers.+)[20]

An animal:

rubēta 'a kind of toad, supposedly poisonous' (Prop.+)

It is immediately obvious that most of the *-ēto-* nouns describe land in some way, most often by what is found in it. Among these, the most common type characterizes a region by its dominant flora, and therefore this is likely to have been the area of earliest productivity.[21]

From the numerous "place where a certain plant grows" words, the use of -*ētum* was extended to name places where other things could be found. One little set is the rocky place words, *saxētum*, *sabulētum*, and *sepulcrētum*. This last is a *hapax*, so it is difficult to determine its possible connotations, but although *sepulcrum* ordinarily refers to the grave or tomb itself, it can also mean the tombstone.[22] Since *sepulcrētum* would otherwise be rather isolated semantically, it seems likely that it was modeled on *saxētum*, which is 'where the stones are', to designate the place 'where the tombstones are'.

When *-ētum* is used to name places where other things are, the words thus created mostly fall into the agricultural sphere. Cattle are to be met with in the *būcētum* and *porcae* 'ridges of soil between furrows' are the distinguishing characteristics of the type of field called a *porculētum*. Two of the *-ētum* nouns are interesting in that they are connected only with adjectives, as opposed to other nouns, and describe areas as having the quality denoted by the adjective: an *asprētum* is a piece of ground that is *asper* and *veterētum* must surely be related to *vetus*, although the noun has a more specific agricultural meaning than merely 'old place'.

Although it is not very difficult to trace the spread of *-ētum* from the plant-place names to the other place designations, this approach does not account for *olīvēta* 'olive-harvest', which is clearly not a place full of olives, but simply a gathering of them. Still less will it explain *acētum*, *tēmētum*, *olētum* 'excrement', and *rubēta*, which apparently have nothing to do with plants or places. These cases do not fit the productive type and therefore may be supposed to shed some light on the earlier history of *-ēto-*.

If we examine these exceptions to the usual pattern, we notice two interesting facts. First, *olīvēta* and *rubēta* are the only non-neuter forms in the entire list.[23] Not only does the appearance of both the feminine and neuter genders suggest that these nouns are really substantivized adjectives, but *rubēta* is actually used as an adjective modifying *rāna*.[24] Furthermore, the gender and meaning of *olīvēta* 'olive-harvest', as opposed to *olīvētum* 'olive-yard', provide an important clue as to the original function of the substantivization. The feminine *ā*-stems in Indo-European are widely believed to have originated as collectives derived from *o*-stems. It is perfectly appropriate, therefore, that a collection of olives should be an *olīvēta*.

Second, *acētum*, *olētum*, and *rubēta* also stand out as the only words in the list that are not synchronically derivable from a nominal form, but rather appear beside stative verbs, namely *aceō*, *oleō*, and *rubeō*, respectively. Let us turn our attention now to these pairs. On any analysis, *acētum*, *olētum*, and *rubēta* seem to be formed from a stem in stative *-ē-* plus a suffix *-to-*. This *-to-* is presumably the same suffix that makes *-to-*participles, but *aceō*, *oleō*, and *rubeō* have no synchronic *-to-*participles attested. In fact, few stative verbs in Latin have *-to-*participles at all. Even when they do exist, these participles seldom, if ever, go back directly to *-ēto-*. In some cases, the *-to-* has been added directly to the root, as in *taedeō*, *taesus* (< **taid-to-*). But in other cases, *taceō* for example, the **to*-participle is *tacitus*, which must be from **-ĕ-to-* (cf. Umbr. **taçez**), not **-ē-to-*. The source of this **-ĕ-to-* is almost certainly the **to*-participles of the causatives/iteratives,[25] since the paradigms of these and the statives fell together in the present due to regular phonological changes.[26]

Acētum, *olētum*, and *rubēta* would, therefore, appear to be isolated relics of a more archaic formation of **to*-participles to *-ē-* statives. If this is so, what should these forms in **-ēto-* have meant? If a man who is *tacitus* is silent and one who is *cautus* (< **kauĕto-*) is wary, then something that is *acētum* is sharp or sour, which is a fitting description of vinegar. Likewise, *olētum* is something that is (foul-)smelling. Hence, it is very likely that the *rubēta* is red.

The agreement of Umbr. **taçez** with Lat. *tacitus* suggests that **-ēto-* was being replaced by **-ĕ-to-* already in Italic, but the fact remains that, for many statives, Latin preserves no **to*-participle at all. One might wonder then, what came to fill that semantic role? There seem to be two options in many cases. One is the *nt*-participle; since *to*-participles of statives only rarely convey any sense of past time or passivity, *tacitus* is essentially synonymous with *tacens* and *acētum* with *acens*, *olētum* with *olens*,[27] etc. The other option is an adjective in *-idus*. These adjectives are quite productive in Latin in this function and *acidus*, *olidus*, and *rūbidus* are attested.

Tēmētum is most likely modeled on *acētum*; both are fluids ingested by people and both are also probably grape-derived in most cases.[28] *Acētum* may also have influenced *cocētum*, which Festus defines as "*genus edulii ex melle et papavere factum*". As mentioned above, *cocētum* is thought to be adapted from Gk. κυκεών, which refers to a drink made from wine, as well as honey or other ingredients to taste, and so the *-ētum* may have been added to the Greek stem when the word was borrowed into Latin, since it referred to another grape-derived beverage. If the substance later came to be thought of as a foodstuff, rather than a thick drink, or if the name *cocētum* was transferred to a different, more solid, concoction altogether, the formant may then have spread to the other two dishes, *morētum* and *tuccētum*.

Olētum 'excrement' must have been the starting-point for *fimētum* and *olenticētum*. *Olētum* is certainly a substance spoken of as a collective, and therefore there is not much to distinguish between dung, a dung-heap, and a place that smells foul (possibly because dung is prevalent).

Only a few of the attested nouns, however, can be analyzed as stative *-ē-* plus **-to-*. Most numerous are the words for clumps of trees or other plants and it is from these that *-ētum* has been extended to certain other sorts of places, as discussed above. But the morphology of the stative derivatives of the *acētum*-type and of the productive place names is the same. It is very tempting, therefore, to look for a way in which the two can be connected.

There does appear to be one point of contact; *rubēto- appears in two of the semantic categories listed above, as the toad called *rubēta* and as the place where the *rubus* grows, the *rubētum*. While it is true that neither of these particular words is attested very early, nevertheless they should be quite old, since they show positive evidence of the adjectival origins of the *-ēto- nouns and are also among the few that can be matched with a verb in stative -ē-. It has already been shown that *rubēta rāna* should literally mean 'red toad'. By the same token, *rubētum* should, in the first instance, have meant 'red thing'.

Now *rubus* can mean both the blackberry and the prickly shrub on which it grows. Of course, despite the English name, the color of the fruit in question plausibly falls within the range of the root $*h_1reud^h$-. *Rubus* itself goes back to $*(h_1)rud^h$-o- and is likely to be old, since it has an exact cognate in Lith. *rùdas* 'brownish-red'.[29] The sequence of events can be imagined in the following way. The substantivized adjective *rubētum* was adopted as a word for a patch of 'red stuff' consisting of one or more bramble-bushes covered with their reddish fruit. Once established in this usage, *rubētum* naturally became associated with *rubus* more than *rubeō*, given that Latin no longer had participles in *-ē-to- as real synchronic parts of the paradigms of ē-stative verbs.[30] When the connection to *rubeō* ceased to be perceived, the -*ētum* could not be analyzed as consisting of the stative -ē- and the suffix *-to-, and the complex could then be segmented off and used freely as a suffix-like unit itself.

From *rubētum*, the spread of -*ētum* to other clumps of plant-life can be traced. Although the most common subset is the group derived from the names of trees, among the other plants a significant number are types of thorn-bushes: *dumētum*, *rosētum*, *spinētum*, and *senticētum*, not to mention *rubētum* itself. This group accounts for very nearly half of the non-tree plants and this fact would seem to lend some support to the idea that *rubētum* was the original model for the type.

Finally, the growing popularity of -*ētum*, in agricultural terminology especially, and particularly the influence of *vīnētum*, seem to have prompted the creation of *fūnētum* and *masculētum*, which, however, do not fit the general pattern of meaning.

It will have been noticed that a few words, namely *olenticētum*, *senticētum*, and *būcētum*, show an expanded formant -*cētum*. This would appear to have been extracted from cases where the sequence arose from the addition of -*ētum* to a velar stem, as in *fruticētum* (from *frutex*), *īlicētum* (*īlex*), *nucētum* (*nux*), *quercētum* (*quercus*), *fīcētum* (*fīcus*), and *iuncētum* (*iuncus*). From such cases -*cētum* could have been mis-segmented, although it is difficult to see why, since the velar in each case clearly belongs to the name of the plant.

To return now to *Monēta*, some modern scholars, such as Vaniček, have suggested that this might be a formation like *rubēta*. Walde-Hofmann, on the other hand, reject the notion that *Monēta* can be derived from *moneō* at all, because the formation is proper only to statives, not causatives like *moneō*.³¹ But while it is undeniable that such a deverbative from a causative cannot have been inherited, it is nevertheless true that the statives and causatives in Latin have influenced each other analogically in many ways. We have already seen how participles like *tacitus* were modeled on those of the causative/iteratives. The analogy can also work in the opposite direction. For example, verbs of the type *commonefaciō* and *condocefaciō* are made from the causatives *moneō* and *doceō* on the model of another formation proper to the statives, cf. *calefaciō* and *caleō*, *arefaciō* and *areō*.³² Therefore, it is perfectly possible that *Monēta* may have been created analogically from *moneō* on the model of *rubēta* : *rubeō*, etc.

Finally, granted that such a creation is analogically possible, what would it mean? If *Monēta* stands in the same relation to *moneō* as *acētum*, *rubēta*, and the others do to *aceō*, *rubeō*, etc., then it should be functionally equivalent to a present participle. Therefore *Monēta* should be the one who reminds, i.e., the memory. Recall the passage of Varro: *is qui monet, proinde sit ac memoria*; the semantic fit is unexceptionable. The analogy thus provides a reasonable Latin name for Μνημοσύνη.

NOTES

1. *Od.* 27, 14 W.
2. *B. P.* 54, 46 W.
3. *Ann.* 428 W.
4. See Cicero, *Div.* 1.101.
5. Other causatives of this structure in Latin include *doceō* and *noceō*.
6. *L. L.* 49: *Meminisse a memoria, cum <in> id quod remansit in mente rursus movetur; ... Ab eodem monere, quod is qui monet, proinde sit ac memoria.*
7. *Memoria* is rather from the root *(s)mer-*, cf. Skt. *smarate* 'remembers'.
8. See *Div.* 2.69 (*Quod item dici de Moneta potest*; *a qua praeterquam de sue plena quid umquam moniti sumus?*), refering back to the story told in 1.101. Compare also Isidore of Seville, 16.18.8.
9. The definitions are taken from the *OLD*, except where otherwise noted.
10. This would be a feminine variant of *myrtētum* and occurs only at *Vid.* 93 (*nescio qui servos e myrteta prosilit*). The feminine may be genuinely old (For more on nouns in *-ēta*, see below.) or may have arisen as a misinterpretation of the neuter nom. and acc. pl. The *OLD* suggests that Priscian has simply misquoted the text.
11. It is somewhat interesting to note that each of the doublets *olea* and *olīva*, both meaning 'olive-tree' and 'olive' has its own *-ētum* noun.
12. This must be a place where the *salix* grows, and so the extra *-t-* before *-ētum* is presumably the result of a contamination between the expected **salicētum* and the synonymous *salictum*.
13. On the placement of *sepulcrētum* in this group, see the discussion of the semantic categories below.
14. This word has a by-form, *būcītum*, and therefore may not really belong here.

15. It may be interesting to note that this is apparently derived from a diminutive, not independently attested, of *porca* 'balk', which happens to end up looking identical to the word for 'female pig'.
16. Definition of Lewis and Short. The *OLD* does not give one, simply refering to the sole quotation.
17. For the most part, these words will not be taken into account in the following discussion. As will be seen from the note on each, their etymologies are not very clear and at least two of the three appear to be borrowings.
18. Definition of Lewis and Short. The *OLD* cites the definition from Paul. *Fest.*: *genus edulii ex melle et papavere factum*. This word is said to be, at least in its stem, a borrowing from Greek related to κυκάω 'stir, mix' (LSJ) and κυκεών "'potion, posset' ... containing barley-groats, grated cheese, and Pramnian wine (*Il.*), also honey and magical drugs (*Od.*)" (LSJ). The stem-vowel was changed to *-o-* in Latin under the influence of *coquō*, according to W-H; O. Keller, *Lateinische Volksetymologie und Verwandtes* (Leipzig, 1891), p. 81.
19. The etymology of this word is unclear. Most often it is said to be from a root **mer-*, meaning something like 'to rub', which is supposed to be the root of Lat. *mortārium* and, with a "*d*-extension", *mordeō*.
20. According to a scholiast on Pers. 2.42, this dish is made from marinated beef or pork. It is said to be a Gaulish loan-word and possibly related to an Umbrian word *toco* that may mean 'salted'.
21. These words have almost the feel of technical terms; many appear for the first time in the works of Cato, Varro, Columella, and Pliny.
22. E.g. Cic. *Sen.* 7.21 ... *nec sepulcra legens vereor* ...
23. I except the possibly erroneous *myrtēta*, on which see above.
24. E.g. Prop. 3.6.27.
25. The **to*-participles of the causatives/iteratives are themselves analogical to verbs of the *capiō* type. The proportion was $*kap\text{-}i^e/_o : *kap\text{-}to\text{-} :: *mon\text{-}e\text{-}i^e/_o : X = *mon\text{-}e\text{-}to\text{-}$.
26. Jasanoff, p. 66.
27. See *OLD olens*, meaning b, 'rank, stinking'.
28. The etymology of *tēmētum* is otherwise obscure; its only clear relative is *abstēmius*.
29. Cf. also OE *rudu* 'red color' < $*(h_1)rud^h\text{-}\bar{a}$.
30. Notice that Pliny believes that the *rubēta* toad also takes its name from *rubus*, rather than *rubeō* (*Nat.* 32.50: *sunt quae in vepribus tantum vivunt, ob id rubetarum nomine* ...).
31. W-H also object on the grounds that words of the *acētum*-type are all neuter, with the exceptions of *rubēta* and *valētūdō*. Note that *valētūdō* does not necessarily presuppose a lost **valēta* beside *valēre*, *valēscō*, but may be analogical to other cases where a noun in *-ētūdō* is found beside a verb in *-ēre* or *-ēscere*. There are a few such cases: *alētūdō* : *alēscō*, *inquiētūdō* : *quiēscō*, *as-*, *con-*, *dē-*, and *mansuētūdō* : *as-*, *con-*, *dē-*, and *mansuēscō*. Nevertheless, *rubēta* certainly exists.
32. Jasanoff, p. 121.

33
homōnēs

Od. 33 W: *Topper facit homones ut prius fuerunt,*

Warmington here prints the emendation *homones*, for *homines*, suggested by C. O. Müller. This emendation has been accepted by few, if any, other editors; Morel, Mariotti, and Verrusio, for example, all keep *homines* in the text.[1]

In addition to the familiar stem *homĭn-* (< **homŏn-*[2]), Ennius does preserve an accusative *homōnem* (*Ann.* 141 W).[3] Since both *homōn-* and **homŏn-* are attested in old Latin and since Latin has both patterns, those with a short stem vowel (e.g., *virgō, virgĭnis*) and those with a long (e.g., *sermō, sermōnis*), it is difficult to say which may have been the original inflection in this particular word.

Osc. **humuns** '*homines*' (nom. pl.) and Umbr. *homonus* '*hominibus*' (dat.-abl. pl.) are standardly said to be stems in *-ōn-*.[4] Yet in both cases, the vowel of the suffix is spelled with precisely the same character as the vowel in the first syllable, which is unequivocally a short *-ŏ-*. It is perfectly possible, then, that Osc. **humuns** and Umbr. *homonus* both go back to a stem **homŏn-*. Furthemore, in Oscan and, less regularly, in Umbrian, a long *-ō-* tends to be spelled *-u-* in the Latin alphabet.[5] Finally, the fact that the *-o-* has not been syncopated is no indication that it is long. There are several parallels to suggest that short vowels in medial open syllables can be maintained or restored under the influence of unsyncopated forms within the same paradigm. For example, the Oscan nominative singular **meddíss** has had this effect on the genitive **medíkeís** and dative **medíkeí**. Such retention or restoration is quite regular in the participles in **-ĕ-to-*, e.g., Umbr. *tasetur* '*tacitī*' and **maletu** '*molitum*'.[6]

The only other form that is now cited as evidence that Italic had a *-ō-* throughout the stem of the word for 'man' is the South Picene dative singular *nemúneí* (TE 5), which Marinetti and others have connected with Lat. *nēminī*.[7] *Nemúneí*, written with the modified *ú*-sign which regularly indicates a *-ō-* in inscriptions where the alphabet distinguishes,[8] is said to preserve the older inflection in *-ōn-*, along with Ennius' *homōnem*, versus the *-ŏn-* of *nēminī*, which is said to be a Latin innovation.

While *nemúneí* certainly seems to have a long *-ō-* in its stem, the form is not reliable evidence for the Italic inflection of 'man'. First, the context of the inscription does not make it at all certain that *nemúneí* is to be translated '*nēminī*'. It is used in apposition to the dative singular *mefistrúí*[9] and may just as well be, as Eichner takes it, a proper name.[10] Furthermore, if *nemúneí* is from **nĕ + hemōn-*, as Marinetti suggests, one might reasonably expect a long *-ē-* contraction product to be written with the modified *-i-*sign, rather than the *e-*sign normally used for a short *-ĕ-*. Since *nemúneí* cannot, with any certainty, be connected to *hemō/homō* at all, it is irrelevant to this discussion.

Nevertheless, Vine, taking the Oscan, Umbrian, and South Picene forms as evidence of an Italic **homōn-*, has suggested that Latin inherited *homōn-*, but replaced it with *homĭn-* under the influence of *virgĭn-*, as the only other plain *n*-stem for an animate being.[11] Although the Oscan and Umbrian are not proof of an Italic **homōn-*, it cannot be ruled out as a starting point. But the pressure of the single word, *virgĭn-*, and a feminine one at that, is not a very satisfactory motivating force.

If, on the other hand, we assume for the moment that *homĭn-* continues the original inflection, we must ask, what could have induced a shift to *-ōn-*? There can be little doubt that *-ōn-* is a productive stem type in Latin, for example, in the large class of abstract nouns in *-tiō, -tiōnis*. More relevant for these purposes, however, is the fact that *-ōn-* seems to have been quite productive in the creation of words for people of various occupations or characters, e.g., *caupōn-* 'inn-keeper', *lēnōn-* 'procurer', *mūliōn-* 'muleteer', *equisōn-* 'groom', *agāsōn-* 'groom, driver', *errōn-* 'truant', etc. Therefore, there would appear to have been considerable pressure in the direction of *-ōn-*, which could have introduced *homōn-* as a by-form of an older *homŏn-*.

If *homōn-* had been the original form, one might rather have expected this semantic class of persons in *-ōn-* to have reinforced the old inflection. Yet *homōn-* does not, in fact, survive into classical Latin. Thus, if *virgĭn-* had any influence at all, it seems that, rather than cause *homĭn-* to oust an older *homōn-*, *virgĭn-* may have helped to preserve *homĭn-* against the weight of the increasing mass of substantives in *-ōn-*. In any case, *homōn-* would appear to be a trace of an innovation begun in old Latin that simply did not catch on.

In addition to these two inflections of *homō*, an accusative singular *hemonem* is cited in Paul. *Fest.* (p. 100 M). Furthermore, *nēmō* is standardly taken to be the result of a contraction of *nĕ + hemō*, which would provide indirect evidence for the by-form. Whether or not this is the correct interpretation of *nēmō* will be discussed below, but, given that Festus does preserve the one form, there can be little doubt that *hemō* existed. The question is, what is the relationship between *hemō* and *homō*? Toward this end, it will be useful first to examine the etymology and morphology of *homō*.

Homō is derived from the IE word for 'earth' $*d^h\acute{e}\hat{g}^h\text{-}ōm$ (Gk. χθών, Hitt. *tekan*), which made a locatival form $*d^h\hat{g}^h\text{-}m\text{-}\acute{e}n$ 'on earth' (Skt. *jmán*). It has been convincingly shown that a derivative, $*d^h\hat{g}^h\text{-}m\text{-}\breve{o}n\text{-}$ '(living) on earth, earthling', made from this locative is the pre-form of Lith. *žmuõ* (< $*d^h\hat{g}^h\text{-}m\text{-}ō$) and Go., OE *guma*, etc. (< $*d^h\hat{g}^h\text{-}m̥m\text{-}ō$).[12]

Lat. *hemō* has been explained as an *e*-grade variant of this derivative and is often believed to be a genuine archaism,[13] while *homō* has long been taken as a phonological development of *hemō* according to a putative Latin sound change of -*ĕ*-to-*ŏ*- before an -*o*- in the following syllable.[14] Recently, however, the environment for such a sound change has been demonstrated by Schrijver to be considerably narrower than this one given in the older literature.[15] A more precise formulation would be, -*ĕ*- became -*ŏ*- following a labial consonant and preceding a nasal consonant that is followed by another -*o*-.[16] Therefore, since *h*- is clearly not a labial consonant, this rule cannot apply. In short, there is no way for the -*ŏ*- of *homō* to be a phonological development of -*ĕ*- in this position. Furthermore, it cannot be demonstrated that the -*e*- of *hemō* is, in fact, short at all; the only direct attestation is that of Festus, and *nēmō* could, of course, equally well reflect *ně* + *hēmō* as *ně* + *hěmō*.

If, however, *hemō* does have a short -*ĕ*-, it could be quite an old form derived from yet another locative of the word for 'earth'. In addition to *jmán*, Sanskrit also has a locative singular *kṣám-i* < *$d^h\hat{g}^h$-ém-i*, whose *e*-grade suffix might ultimately account for the vocalism of *hemō*.[17]

On the whole, though, it would be preferable if the vocalism of the Latin, Oscan, and Umbrian forms could be reconciled with the zero-grade of their Germanic and Baltic cognates. Vine has suggested that the Italic forms do, in fact, go back to a zero-grade pre-form and that Latin (or Italic) *hom*- is the regular outcome of *$d^h\hat{g}^h$-m̥(m)-*.[18]

There is little to contradict the idea that *-m̥(m)*- gave -*ŏm*-. The immediate pre-form of the Latin superlative suffix -*i(s)simo*- is sometimes given as *-isămo*- from *-ism̥mo*-,[19] but the only evidence for an *-ă*- stage is in Celtic, e.g., MW *hynhaf* (lit. 'oldest', = OIr. *sinem*) < *senisămo*-. As Vine correctly points out, Lat. -*i(s)simo*- can perfectly well reflect *-isŏmo*- from *-ism̥mo*-.

With this we may compare the explanation of Lat. *sum* and Osc. **súm** 'I am' offered by B. Joseph and R. Wallace.[20] According to their theory, the inherited *esmi* (< *$h_1$es-mi*) was apocopated in proto-Italic and the resulting *esm̥* developed first to *esəm*, and thence to *esom*.[21] *Sum* and **súm** would both result from the generalization of the enclitic by-form *səm (and compare enclitic third singular *st* beside orthotone *est* in Lat. *vocitatust* (*CIL* 1.199.17) and Osc. **destrst** '*dextrā est*'.[22] If such a secondary syllabic *-m̥*- gave *-om*- already in Italic, as Joseph and Wallace suggest, *-m̥(m)*- is very likely to have had the same outcome.

One other possible example of this change of *-m̥*- to -*om*- is Umbr. **sumel**, which is synonymous, and presumably cognate, with Lat. *simul*. *Simul*[23] 'at the same time' would appear to be from the paradigm of the adjective *similis* (< *semili*-).[24] The old neuter nominative-accusative singular of *similis* would have been *sem-(i)li*, which underwent apocope to give *seml̥*. A secondary syllabic -*l̥*- of this sort regularly develops to *-əl and ultimately -ul in Latin, cf. *facul* 'easily' (< **fakəl* < **fakli*), the old neuter of *facilis*. Umbr. **sumel** seems very likely to be a neuter nominative-accusative singular form of the adjective **sem-(i)li-* also, but it cannot go back directly to **semli-* with a root *e*-grade. The surface *o*-vocalism of **sumel** can best be accounted for by reconstructing a zero-grade variant **sm̥l(i)* of the pre-form that gives Lat. *simul*.²⁵ This development of **sm̥-* to *som-* in Umbr. **sumel** would be further evidence that *-m̥-* became *-om-* already in Italic.

If then *hemō* does not actually go back to anything inherited, and there is nothing comparable to it elsewhere in Italic, how could it have been created within Latin? The only likely source for it would appear to be *nēmō*. It is conceivable that from *nēmō* an antonymous **ēmō* could have been backformed on the model of *nullus* 'none' and *ullus* 'any'.²⁶ The initial *h-* would, very naturally, have been added, giving *hēmō*, for the simple reason that *homō* was spelled so. In neither word was the *h-* likely to have been pronounced anyway. If this scenario is correct, the *-e-* of *hēmō* must perforce be long, which, as discussed above, is perfectly possible.²⁷

If *hēmō* was drawn in some way from *nēmō*, it follows then that *nēmō* itself cannot be the result of contracting *nĕ* and *hemō*, but could simply be the phonologically regular result of the univerbation of *nĕ* and *homō*.²⁸ There seems to be no evidence to disprove that *-ĕ- + -ŏ-* would regularly contract to *-ē-*, but neither are there any positive examples of such a contraction. The paradigm of the causative verbs in *-ei̯e/o-* should show the treatment of this sequence; for example, the first person plural of *monēre* should go back to **mon-ei̯o-mos*. If *monēmus* were the direct phonological outcome of this pre-form, *nēmō* could simply be from *nĕ* + *homō*. But it cannot be proven that *monēmus* is directly from **mon-ei̯o-mos*; it is just possible that *monēmus* is an analogical replacement of whatever **mon-ei̯o-mos* did give, modeled on the corresponding form of the other major component of the Latin second conjugation, the presents in the familiar stative *-ē-*. This *-ē-* is itself not a contraction product at all, but an inherited *-ē-*. It is conceivable that, once the paradigms of the causatives and statives began to overlap by regular sound change,²⁹ any remaining differences were leveled out by spreading *-ē-* throughout both paradigms, thereby collapsing them into a single conjugation. Nevertheless, there is no way to rule out *-ē-* as the contraction product of *-ĕ-* and *-ŏ-*.

Hēmō can thus be explained as a by-form of *homō* created from its opposite, *nēmō*, which is itself most likely a contraction of *nĕ* and *homō*. Of the two stems **homŏn-* and *homōn-*, the former must be the older. The evidence for a long *-ō-* in Italic is entirely inconclusive; the spelling of Osc. **humuns** and Umbr. **homonus** is ambiguous at best, while the context of SPi. **nemúneí** (plus the apparent short *-ĕ-* in the initial syllable) makes the equation with *nēminī* dubious. Furthermore, *homōn-* can easily have been analogically created within Latin beside an older **homŏn-*, whereas there is no good analogical model for the creation of a secondary *homŏn- from an older homōn-.

Homōn- is an example of an old Latin innovation that did not persist into the classical language, but that alone is not a compelling reason to emend the transmitted reading *homines* in Livius. There is every reason to believe *homōn-* to be the later of the two inflections, and no evidence of its existence before Ennius. The text of Livius is, therefore, best left unemended.

NOTES

1. Mariotti (p. 99) cites *homines* in Naevius (*B.P.* 18 W) as support.
2. Cf. the diminutive *homullus* < *homŏn-elo-*.
3. The fragment is quoted by Priscian, *ap. G. L.*, II.206.22 K: *Vetustissimi 'homo homonis' declinaverunt*.
4. For example, at Buck *OU*, § 181.b. See also Untermann, p. 329 f.
5. Buck *OU*, § 53, 54.
6. Buck *OU*, § 88.2.
7. See Marinetti (p. 118), who considers the -ō- to have been extended from the nominative singular, and Vine (p. 245).
8. Cf., also in TE 5, the nominative plural *safinús* [-ōs] '**Sabini**'. AP 2, on the other hand, uses both the *o*-sign and the *ú*-sign, but there seems to be at least one case of -*ú*- representing an etymological -ŏ-, in the accusative singular *meitimúm* (Marinetti, p. 90).
9. A comparative (*mef-is-tero-*) from the root *medʰ-* of Lat. *medius*, according to Marinetti (p. 121). What this would mean in this context is also unclear; Eichner seems to take it as an epithet or title, although he proposes a different etymology (*Die Sprache* [1988] p. 200).
10. *Op. cit.*, p. 199.
11. p. 245.
12. Nussbaum, p. 187 ff.
13. Vine, p. 244, with reference to Nussbaum, p. 187 ff.
14. See, for example, Sommer, § 79 and L-H, § 111.
15. Schrijver, *The Reflexes of the Proto-Indo-European Laryngeals in Latin*, p. 466 ff. and Vine, p. 246.
16. In some handbooks, such as L-H, examples of this sound change and of the regular change of ĕl > ŏl are both listed under this so-called "*o*-umlaut" rule.
17. For a detailed account, see Nussbaum, p. 187 ff.
18. p. 247 ff.
19. Sihler (p. 367), for example, sets up a stage *-isămo- for Italic.
20. *AJP* 108 (1987), p. 675–93.
21. Joseph and Wallace suggest that this secondary *-m̥- developed to -ŏm- phonologically, although they do not rule out the possibility that *esəm had its ending replaced with the seconday thematic ending *-om.
22. See Buck *OU*, § 84.
23. *Semol* (*CIL* 1.2.1531), *semul* (Pl. *Ba.* 576, 577, 591; *Ci.* 770; *Men.* 405; *Mer.* 689).
24. For the raising of ĕ ... i > ī ... i, cf. *cinis* < *kenis (cf. Gk. κόνις).

25. It is phonologically possible that Umbr. **sumel** simply has a root *o*-grade like Gk. ὁμαλός 'even, equal' (see Meiser, p. 59), but whereas ὁμαλός is quite possibly an inner-Greek creation from ὁμός 'same', the *o*-grade is otherwise unattested in Italic.
26. *Nullus*, when refering a person, and *nēmō* were so nearly synonymous that the gen. *nullius* and abl. *nullō* came to replace *nēminis* and *nēmine* (both found, for example, in Plautus) in the synchronic paradigm of *nēmō* in classical Latin.
27. Another possible scenario, but one that would probably yield -*ĕ*- in *hemō*, is that *hemō* was extracted from a variant spelling *nehemō* for *nēmō* (*cf. prĕhendo* vs. *prendō*), which was reanalyzed as composed of the privative *nĕ*- (as in *nescius*, *nefas*, etc.) plus a *hemō* synonymous with *homō*. However, there is no evidence that *nēmō* was ever spelled this way.
28. See also Vine, p. 244.
29. E.g., in the second and third persons singular, *monēs* (< *$mon\text{-}éi̯e\text{-}si$*) and *monet* (< *$monēt$* < *$mon\text{-}éi̯e\text{-}ti$*) end up looking just like *rubēs* (*$(h_1)rud^h\text{-}ē\text{-}s$*) and *rubet* (< *$rubēt$* < *$(h_1)rud^h\text{-}ē\text{-}t$*).

39
gāvīsī

Od. 39 W: '*quoniam audivi, paucis gavisi*;

This fragment was preserved because it shows *gāvīsī*, a non-deponent perfect of *gaudēre*, for classical *gāvīsus sum*. Priscian attributes *gāvīsī* to the most archaic writers,[1] but this is the only example of such a perfect in attested Latin and the deponent perfect is found as early as Terence (*Hau.* 857).

This situation of early non-deponent vs. classical deponent perfect is paralleled by *audēre*, for which *ausī* is once attested (Cato, *Orat.* 199) for the usual *ausus sum*.[2] Both *gāvīsī* and *ausī* are somewhat suspect, partly because of their very limited attestation, but more importantly because they are descriptively *s*-perfects. The significance of this fact depends on an analysis of the morphology of *gaudēre* and *audēre*, to which we shall now turn.

Audēre 'to dare' is apparently a denominative present in the familiar stative -*ē*- made from the adjective *avidus* 'eager', and has undergone syncope from *$au̯idē$- to $au̯dē$-.[3] *Gaudēre*, as well, seems likely to be a denominative to an adjective in -*idus*, although *$gāvidus$ is unattested. *Gaudēre* is standardly referred to the root *geh_2-, from which at least two presents were made in Greek. One is Hom. γαίω 'rejoice' < *geh_2-u-$i̯e/o$-, with a "*u*-extended" form of the root that could also underlie *geh_2-u-$id^h o$- > *$gau̯ido$-. It would seem, then, that *$gau̯ido$- is an -*idus* adjective associated with a lost Latin *$gāu̯ere$, cf., e.g., *candidus* : *candēre*. Thus *$gāu̯ere$ and γαίω would fit a recognized pattern in which Latin (and Baltic) *ē*-statives correspond to synonymous -$i̯e/o$- verbs in Greek and Indo-Iranian.[4] The other Greek present is γηθέω/γᾱθέω 'rejoice' < *geh_2-d^h-, with an added -d^h- which one is tempted to associate also with *gaudēre*.[5] If the appearance of a -d^h- in γηθέω and *gaudēre* is not coincidental, the hypothetical *$gau̯ido$- may not be an ordinary adjective in -*idus* at all; rather the -*i*- and the -*u*- of *$gau̯ido$- may be of the type found in, for example, Gk. δολιχός 'long' (< *$dl̥h_1$-i-$g^h o$-), on the one hand, and Hitt. *daluka*- 'long' (< *$dl̥h_1$-u-$g^h o$-), on the other. It seems somewhat odd, however, that *$gau̯ido$- should have both a -*u*- and an -*i*- of this sort, rather than one or the other, as with the Greek and Hittite examples above. It is probably better, therefore, to take the *-d^h- (> -*d*-) of *$gau̯ido$- as belonging to the *-i-$d^h o$- suffix after all, even at the cost of separating the *-d^h- of *gaudēre* from the *-d^h- (> -t^h-) of γηθέω. Whatever the ultimate history of *$gau̯ido$-, it seems to have served, like ordinary -*idus* adjectives, as the basis of a denominative stative.

It is to be noted that *gāvīsus* and, presumably, *gāvīsī* have a long -*ī*- that cannot be phonological, if these are simply from **gau̯id^h-to-* and **gau̯id^h-s-*. There is, however, an obvious analogical source for *gāvīsus* at least; it would appear to have been modeled on *vīsus* at a time, before syncope, when the present **gāvidēre* could be superficially identified with *vidēre*. Given this explanation of *gāvīsus*, one might expect the same analogy to have produced a perfect **gāvīdī*. The absence of **gāvīdī*, coupled with the rarity of *gāvīsī*, makes one suspect that *gāvīsī* was in fact made from *gāvīsus* itself and, therefore, is not the more archaic form.

It is somewhat curious that **avidēre* did not go through the same analogical process(es) and receive a *to*-participle **avīsus* and a perfect **avīsī* (or **au̯īdī*). One possible explanation is that the infectum forms of **avidē-* had already been syncopated, thus effacing any surface resemblance to *vidēre*, even before **gāvidē-* was fitted out with its analogical perfectum. Thus the sequence of events would seem to have been: first, the forms of **avidē-* were syncopated; second, the analogy *vidēre* : **gāvidēre* : : *vīsus* : X produced *gāvīsus* (and therefrom, at some point, *gāvīsī*); third, the forms of **gāvidī-* were syncopated. It is conceivable that the difference in the timing of these two episodes of syncope was conditioned by the length of the vowel in the preceding syllable. This would be comparable to the situation to be discussed in the comment on *pullus* 'dark', below.

NOTES

1. ap. *G.L.*, II.482.9: *Vetustissimi . . . gavisi pro gavisus sum protulerunt*.
2. The deponent perfect is found at least as early as Pacuvius (*tr.* 345 W).
3. The root, **h₁eu̯H-*, is that of Lat. *avēre* 'to be eager', Skt. *ávati* 'promote'.
4. The best examples to compare are Lat. *manēre* vs. Av. (*fra*) *manyeinte*, Lat. *merērī* vs. Gk. μείρομαι, and probably Lat. *horrēre* vs. Skt. *hṛṣyati*. For correspondences between Baltic *ē*-verbs and Indo-Iranian *-i^e/_o*-stems, see W. Schmid, *Studien zum Baltischen und Indogermanischen Verbum* (Weisbaden, 1963). See also my comment on *Morta*.
5. cf. Toch. *kātk-* 'rejoice' < **-d^h-sk̂-*.

40
pulla

Od. 40 W: *vestis pulla purpurea ampla*

Pullus 'dark' is worthy of a brief note because it is one of a very few words that show the treatment of an original -*lu̯*- in Latin. The root is that of Gk. πολιός 'grey' and πελιός 'livid, dark', both from *-i-u̯o-*, cf. also Myc. *po-ri-wa* (neut. nom.-acc. pl.), which shows that the hiatus is the result of a lost intervocalic -*u̯*-. But *pullus* cannot go back to **pol-i-u̯o-* as well. Latin had a prehistoric episode of syncope that eliminated a short vowel between a resonant and -*u̯*-, when a short vowel preceded the resonant ($\breve{V} > \emptyset$ / $\breve{V}L\_u̯V$, where L stands for any resonant). A secondary -*lu̯*- resulting from this syncope simply remained, as in *solvō* < **se-lu̯u̯e/o-* (cf. *luō*, Gk. λύω), and did not assimilate to -*ll*-. Therefore, *pullus* would appear to have the -*u̯o-* suffix, common in adjectives of color,[1] attached directly to the root. For **pol-u̯o-* beside **poli-u̯o-*, compare, for example, **h₁rudʰ-ro-* (> Gk. ἐρυθρός, Lat. *ruber*), beside **h₁rudʰi-ro-* (> Skt. *rudhira-*).

This development can also be observed in *palleō* 'be pale' and its relations, *pallidus*, *pallor*, etc. These are derived from a stem **pal-u̯o-*, which also gives Gmc. **falwa-* 'pale, yellow' (> OE *fealo* 'reddish-yellow', ON *fǫlr* 'pale') and Lith. *palvas* 'pale, pale yellow'.

The only other good instance of -*ll*- from -*lu̯*- involves still another color. A certain type of Roman shoe, distinguished by its red color, was called a *mulleus*. This would appear to be a derivative of a stem cognate with Lith. *mulvas* 'reddish, yellowish'.

After a preceding long vowel, a short vowel between a resonant and -*u̯*- was also syncopated ($\breve{V} > \emptyset$ / $\bar{V}L\_u̯V$), but at a later date than when a short vowel preceded. For example, *bēlva* 'beast' *mīlvus* 'kite', and *pēlvis* 'basin' still scan as three syllables (*bēlŭu̯a*, *mīlŭu̯us*, *pēlŭu̯is*) in early verse, so that this syncope can be dated within the historical period.[2]

NOTES

1. Cf. *flāvus* 'reddish-yellow, golden', *furvus* 'black, dark', etc.
2. Instances of the trisyllabic scansion can be found at Pl. *Rud.* 543 (*bēlva*), *Poe.* 1292 (*mīlvos*), and Laberius 94 (Ribbeck) (*pēlvim*). See also L-H, § 141.b.α.

41
mandisset

Od. 41 W: '*cum socios nostros Ciclops impius mandisset,*

This fragment is cited by Priscian as evidence that the perfect of *mandō, mandere* 'chew' is *mandī*. He adds, however, that some people would say that it is *manduī* and still others *mandidī*.[1]

Since *mandī* is the only one of the three genuinely attested, it is almost certainly the real form. No other examples of the perfect exist,[2] except in Charisius gram., who also gives *mandī* as the form.[3] The other two possibilities mentioned by Priscian are easily explained as secondary creations.

As for *mandidī*, it is doubtless modeled on the corresponding forms of verbs like *condō* and *vendō*; the analogy would have been *vendere*, etc. : *vendidī*, etc. : : *mandere* : X = *mandidī*.

Manduī is not likely to be the original perfect of *mandere*. Although it has not so clear a model as *mandidī*, *-uī* is, in some sense, a default perfect that frequently takes the place of other types. For example, *convertuit* (*CIL* 8.2532) is found for *convertit* and *reguit* (*CIL* 5.923) for *rexit*.[4] Therefore, it is much simpler to account for *mandī* being remade into *manduī* than the reverse.

The etymology of *mandere* is a more complicated business. The root **menth-* given in Walde-Hofmann cannot be right; for one reason, the root appears to have *a*-vocalism.[5] Since a full-grade is to be expected in a plain thematic verb like *mandere*, the root should probably be set up as **mandʰ-*. Gk. μασάομαι 'chew' would then go back to **m̥ndʰ-i̯e/o-* with a zero-grade of this root.

If this is corrrect, Lat. *mentum* 'chin' must be unrelated to *mandere*. Nothing is, in fact, lost by this, since *mentum* has been quite convincingly connected with another root, namely **men-* 'to project, jut', (cf. Lat. *ēmineō* 'project, stand out' and *mons* 'mountain').[6] Therefore the pre-form of *mentum* can be set up as either **men-to-* or **m̥n-to-*. The latter, however, would have the advantage of also giving directly the group of Germanic cognates meaning 'mouth' (Go. *munþs*, ON *muðr*, OE *mūð*, OHG *mund*), as well as MW *mant* 'jaw, mouth'.

NOTES

1. *ap. G. L.*, II.419.12 K.
2. *TLL:* "*alias perf. non occurit*".
3. p. 246 K: ... *forma est quae perfectum facit secundae personae dempta s littera, velut mando mandis mandi* ...

4. See further, L-H, § 437.I.B; Sommer, § 374.
5. This fact is pointed out by E-M.
6. E-M consider this etymology of *mentum* to be without doubt.

46
dextrābus

Od. 46 W: *deque manibus dextrabus*

Nonius gives this fragment as an example of the use of the alternate *ā*-stem dative-ablative plural ending *-ābus*.[1] It is often said that this ending is most often used in place of *-īs* in order to disambiguate the genders in pairs like *fīliīs* and *fīliābus*.[2] In this case, however, an adjective is inflected with *-ābus*, so gender ambiguity cannot be at issue. What, then, would have been the function of the alternative ending in this situation?

It has been suggested that the use of *-ābus* here is due to the influence of *ambābus*.[3] The theory would seem to be that, since hands tend to come in pairs, *manibus* would frequently be modified by *ambābus*,[4] and hence *-ābus* could have been extended to other adjectives modifying *manibus*.

This argument seems unconvincing for several reasons. First, nowhere else does an adjective take the ending *-ābus* because it is describing *manibus*. Secondly, *manibus ambābus* is attested surprisingly rarely and, it seems, no earlier than Apuleius.[5] Thirdly, it would be odd if *dextrābus* were only formed after the "dual" adjectives *ambābus* and *duābus* precisely in a context where the hands in question are not the two belonging to an individual; obviously no one has two right hands. If the standard association of this fragment with Hom. *Od.* 24.534 (τῶν δ' ἄρα δεισάντων ἐκ χειρῶν ἔπτατο τεύχεα) is correct, as seems likely, the hands are those of the men of Ithaca gathered by Eupeithes to seek vengeance for the killing of the suitors. Another motivation for the form of *dextrābus* should perhaps be sought.

Homer naturally brings to mind metrical considerations, although the Saturnian is, of course, an unstable basis for a theory of this sort. But, whatever the regulating principle(s) of the meter may be, few would dispute the observation that virtually all Saturnian lines can be divided, at a word boundary, into two segments, the first of which contains from five to nine syllables and the second from five to eight.[6] Given that the fragment is from Livius' *Odyssey*, *deque manibus dextrabus* is generally thought to be one such segment.[7] Therefore, as far as the number of syllables in a half-line is concerned, *dextrābus* has no advantage over *dexterīs*; both would give eight syllables. One could add here that a third possible form, *dextrīs*, would also give an acceptable total number of syllables.

Another general tendency of the Saturnian may be observed without committing to a theory of its structure. In addition to the main break in the line, another division was first noticed by Korsch, whose original formulation of the

43

rule was dependent on his own quantitative analysis of the Saturnian. In order to avoid this bias, Cole reformulated the description of the *caesura Korschiana* as follows: "in any half-line that contains seven or more syllables the last three or (more rarely) the last four must be preceded by word end."[8] Thus in the half-line *deque manibus dextrabus*, the *caesura Korschiana* falls between *manibus* and *dextrābus*. Notice that although, by this "rule", *dexterīs* would still appear to be as admissible as *dextrābus*, the other possibility, *dextrīs*, would not be. So far there is still no reason for preferring *dextrābus* over *dexterīs*.

Cole goes on to examine the metrical shapes represented in the parts of the colon before and after the *caesura Korschiana*. He observed that when the second part of the colon has three syllables, those three can be scanned as = − = in over sixty cases, as opposed to thirteen examples of = ⌣ =.[9] *Dextrābus* and *dexterīs* would both be trisyllabic words following the caesura. Either word would seem to be allowable, but the two do differ in the quantity of the medial syllable, where the statistics show a fairly decided preference for a heavy syllable. This is precisely the position in the half-line where *dextrābus* provides a long vowel, whereas *dexterīs*, on the other hand, would give the less desirable short vowel. Therefore it would appear that Livius took advantage of the alternate *ā*-stem dative-ablative plural ending *-ābus*, normally used to disambiguate the gender of substantives, in order to create an adjectival form that would fit a preferred metrical pattern.

NOTES

1. '*Dextrabus*' *pro dexteris*... (493.16).
2. See, for example, L-H, § 350.
3. L-H, § 35 end.
4. Presumably *duābus* would work as well for this scenario.
5. *Manibus duābus* is apparently even rarer and first in Ovid.
6. See T. Cole, "The Saturnian Verse" (*YCS*, 1969), p. 10. I have found this an extremely useful study of this problematic subject and the following discussion is based on some of Cole's findings.
7. Cole, *op. cit.*, p. 17.
8. *Op. cit.*, p. 19.
9. *Op. cit.*, p. 25–28.

Section Two:

Tragedies

4
praeda

tr. 4 W: *Nam ut Pergama
accensa et praeda per participes aequiter
partita est,*

    The root of *praeda* is standardly said to be that of the Latin verb *pre(he)ndō* 'take hold of', but reconciling the noun and verb involves both phonological and morphological problems that are not adequately treated in the handbooks.[1]

    From the time of Plautus onwards, two competing forms of the verb are attested: *prehendō* and *prendō*. At the time of the texts, the distinction is not simply one of spelling; both the monosyllabic stem *prend-* and the disyllabic *prehend-* are metrically guaranteed.[2] The usual explanation of the relationship between the two forms is that *prend-* resulted from contraction after the disappearance of *-h-* from *prehend-*. *Prehend-* itself is said to be composed of the preverb **prai-* and a Latin root set up as **hend-* in purely descriptive terms. This treatment of **prai-* raises certain phonological questions, but the comparative evidence for the verb presents morphological problems to be addressed first.

    No uncompounded form of the verb exists in Latin, but it does have cognates. The descriptive **hend-*, taken with Gk. χανδάνω 'take in, hold, comprise, contain', suggests a root whose consonantal frame is **g^{h}Vnd-*. But whereas **hend-* could be the regular development of either **g^{h}end-* or **g^{h}n̥d-*, the Greek present cannot go back directly to either of these pre-forms, which would give a Greek **k^{h}end-* or **k^{h}ad-* respectively, not **k^{h}and-*.

    Furthermore, χανδάνω has an additional nasal suffix absent from the Latin, although we also find two nasals in the Celtic, OIr. *ro-geinn* 'finds room in' and MW *genni* 'be contained, find room in' (both from a proto-Celtic **g^{h}n̥d-n-*[3]), and some of the Germanic cognates, Go. *du-ginnan* and OE *on-, bi-ginnan*, all meaning 'to begin'.[4] Other Germanic forms, however, lack a nasal entirely; ON *geta* 'to get, obtain; beget', Go. *bi-gitan* 'to find', OE *be-gietan* 'to receive, produce' and *for-gietan* 'to forget' reflect a Germanic stem **geta-*. To account for the cognates both with and without a nasal, Pokorny sets up an IE root with two by-forms, **g^{h}end-* and **g^{h}ed-*. This would be an unusual situation, however, and it would be preferable if the two could be reconciled and all the attested forms derived ultimately from a unitary root.

    It is evidence from within Latin itself that may help clarify this picture. *Praeda* 'booty' is standardly said to be a compound of **prai* (> Lat. *prae*) and a verbal noun from the root of *(pre)hendō* itself. The absence of any *-n-* from this nominal form suggests that the nasal was proper only to the verbal forms and may thus originally have been simply the familiar present-forming infix. The root could therefore be set up as *$*g^hed$-*, which formed a nasal-infix present *$*g^h$-n(e)-d-*.[5] The stem with zero-grade of the infix, *$*g^h$-n̥-d-*, could directly give Lat. **hend-* in the present; the appearance of the *-n-* in the rest of the paradigm (*pre(he)ndī*, *pre(he)nsus*) is simply analogical to the present stem.[6] On the other hand, an inherited present stem *$*g^h$-n(e)-d-* cannot immediately account for Gk. χανδάνω, to which we shall now turn.

Although the present χανδάνω and perfect κέχανδα are made from a *$*k^hand$-*, with invariant *a*-vocalism, this is clearly not the original situation in Greek. The future χείσομαι, shows the familiar digraphic spelling -ει- of a secondary *$*-\bar{e}$-* in Attic and Ionic. Therefore, the future stem is reconstructed as *$*k^h\bar{e}s$-* from *$*k^hend-s$-*, by the second compensatory lengthening.[7] Just as the first -α- of χανδάνω appears to be an innovation, in light of χείσομαι, so too the perfect κέχανδα is secondary given the Homeric κεχόνδει (*Il.* 24. 192), which has the form of a perfect, with reduplication and a characteristic *o*-grade of the "root" *$*k^hend$-*. The thematic aorist (ἐ)χᾰδον would be the regular outcome of a zero-grade *$*k^hn̥d$-*. This points to a synchronic "root" *$*k^hend$-* in proto-Greek with the usual -e/o- ablaut.

The question remains: whence came this Greek "root" *$*k^hend$-?* As we have already seen, the evidence of Lat. *praeda* and Gmc. **geta-* suggests the PIE root was actually *$*g^hed$-*, whose nasal infix present would have been of the shape *$*g^h$-n(e)-d-*. There is good reason to believe, however, that the zero-grade *$*g^hn̥d$-* had a new full-grade *$*g^hend$-* created beside it already in the proto-language. The Gmc. *-ginnan* forms probably go back to *$*g^hend-n$-*, whose additional nasal suffix is reminiscent of Gk. χανδάνω. OIr. *ro-geinn* and MW *genni*, however, can only be reconciled by reconstructing a proto-Celtic *$*g^hn̥d-n$-*,[8] and so provide no positive evidence for the remade form of the root. But the Albanian passive *gjëndem* 'is found', as opposed to *gjej* 'find', seems to be from *$*g^hend$-*.[9] It is even possible that *pre(he)ndō* itself goes back to *$*g^hend$-*, the reflexes of *$*g^hend$-* and *$*g^hn̥d$-* in Latin being indistinguishable. Therefore, it seems that the full-grade *$*g^h$-n(e)-d-* was remodeled to *$*g^h(e)nd$-* within the proto-language.

In Greek, this new "root" *$*g^hend$-* served as the basis of the thematic aorist and the perfect forms. Since the thematic aorist is normally made from the zero-grade of the root (cf. λείπω : ἔλιπον; φεύγω : ἔφυγον), *$*g^hend$-* had the advantage of giving a zero-grade form, *$*g^hn̥d$-*, with a syllabic element, as opposed to the zero-grade *$*g^hd$-* of the original root *$*g^hed$-*. The perfect was remade from the new "root" as well, first still with the *o*-grade preserved in Hom. κεχόνδει.

How, then, was the secondary *a*-vocalism of κέχανδα and of χανδάνω itself introduced? Let us turn first to the morphology of the present stem. χανδάνω is one of a set of Greek verbs that have a thematic present in $*-an^e/_o- < *-n(H)-^e/_o-$.[10] This complex, apparently a thematization of $*-n(e)H-$, also forms presents in Armenian in -ane-, for example *lk'ane-* 'leave', *gtane-* 'find', *harc'ane-* 'ask', and *lizane-* 'lick'.[11] These appear beside what are synchronically thematic aorists, some of which are simply continuations of inherited thematic aorists, such as 3 sg. *elik'* (= Gk. ἔλιπε) and *egit* (= Gk. εἶδε, Skt. *avidat*) beside *lk'ane-* and *gtane-*.[12] Others, however, go back to old imperfects which have been aspectually reclassified in Armenian. Thus the aorist *eharc* is cognate with the Sanskrit imperfect *apṛcchat*, both going back to $*e-pṛk-s^e/_o-$, and *elēz* with the Greek imperfect ἔλειχε. These pairings allow us to define a descriptive rule for Armenian: from a thematic aorist, a present stem can be made by replacing the thematic vowel with the suffix complex $*-n(H)^e/_o-$.

We have already seen that the Greek thematic aorist (ἐ)χάδον goes back to $*g^hn̥d-^e/_o-$ with the zero-grade of the newer "root" $*g^hend-$. If Greek formed present stems from such aorists in the same way as Armenian seems to have done, then the present to $*g^hn̥d-^e/_o-$ would have been $*g^hn̥d-n(H)^e/_o-$, eventually giving *χαδανω, not the actual outcome. But if we compare the other Greek presents in $-an^e/_o-$, we find that quite a few others also show a double nasal, such as μανθάνω, λαμβάνω, λιμπάνω, πυνθάνομαι, λανθάνω, ἀνδάνω, τυγχάνω, and λαγχάνω. It is tempting to say that *χαδανω was remade to χανδάνω in order to conform to this common pattern, but if these presents are, in fact, derived from their aorists, the first nasal in each of these cases is equally unexpected and must therefore be secondary. Also these forms in Greek must be of relatively recent manufacture; witness λιμπάνω beside the still-existing λείπω. Some further elucidation of this class of presents is necessary.

It can be presupposed that Greek and Armenian had inherited the present $*g^hn̥d-n(H)^e/_o-$ (for the IE status of the double-nasal present, compare OIr. *ro-geinn*, etc., discussed above) and the aorist $*g^hn̥d-^e/_o-$ beside pairs of the type $*u̯ind-^e/_o-$: $*u̯id-^e/_o-$ (Skt. *vindati* : *avidat*), as well as presents in $*-n(H)^e/_o-$ like κάμνω $< *km̥-n(H)^e/_o-$, some of which were perhaps already paired with thematic aorists like ἔκαμον. The existence of $*g^hn̥d-n(H)^e/_o-$, and anything else like it that may have been present in the language at that point, made it possible for Greek and Armenian to carry out a common innovation: the $*u̯ind-^e/_o-$-type of present was remade by replacing the thematic vowel with the $*-n(H)^e/_o-$-complex. The two languages later diverged in their treatment of the new double-nasal presents. Greek retains the nasal of both the infix and suffix, for example, in λιμπάνω $< *link^u-n(H)^e/_o-$. But the Armenian cognate, *lk'ane-*, has only the nasal of the suffix. The infix was probably eliminated to clarify the relationship between the present and the aorist, e.g., *lkʻane-* beside *elikʻ*. Thus the Greek and Armenian double-nasal presents seem to have been modeled on the type of $*g^h\eta d\text{-}\eta(H)^e/_o\text{-}$, whose two nasals were present in the proto-language, to judge from the Celtic and Germanic cognates.

Let us now turn to the further history of $*g^h\eta d\text{-}\eta(H)^e/_o\text{-}$ itself in Greek. The double-nasal pattern characteristic of the type of λιμπάνω beside ἔλιπον has been introduced as described above. By regular sound change, then, the present $*g^h\eta d\text{-}\eta(H)^e/_o\text{-}$ became proto-Gk. $*k^h\breve{a}d\text{-}an^e/_o\text{-}$ and the aorist $*g^h\eta d\text{-}^e/_o\text{-}$ became $*k^h\breve{a}d\text{-}^e/_o\text{-}$. The development of the syllabic $*\text{-}\eta\text{-}$ to -ă- left only a single overt nasal in the present with the result that $*k^h\breve{a}d\text{-}an^e/_o\text{-}$ beside the aorist $*k^h\breve{a}d\text{-}^e/_o\text{-}$ no longer conformed to the very pattern it had helped to establish. The situation was easily remedied by analogically inserting a suitable nasal into $*k^h\breve{a}d\text{-}an^e/_o\text{-}$ to give $*k^hand\text{-}an^e/_o\text{-}$ (> χανδάνω). Meanwhile, the perfect stem $*k^he\text{-}k^hond\text{-}$ remained into the historical period, as evidenced by Hom. κεχόνδει. But the -ă- (< $*\text{-}\eta\text{-}$) of χανδάνω and (ἐ)χᾰδον must have suggested that the verb should have *a*-vocalism in the perfect as well, and so it was remade into classical κέχανδα.

To return to Latin, *praeda* is generally agreed to be a verbal abstract in -*ā* from the root $*g^hed\text{-}$ with the preverb/preposition $*pra\underline{i}$, the same elements as *pre(he)ndō*. Even in attested Latin, *praeda* is still found as a verbal abstract, 'the act or practice of plundering'.[13] Cicero pairs it with other abstract nouns in two passages:

> *Comites vero Antoni ... Saxae et Cafoni tradiderunt ad facinus*
> *praedamque natis,* (*Phil.* 11.37)

> *...civitatem Syracusanam propter Heraclii hereditatem non*
> *minus esse isti amicam quam Mamertinam propter praedarum ac*
> *furtorum omnium societatem* (*Ver.* II.4.136).

This juxtaposition with *facinus* in the first passage and *furtōrum* in the second confirms that *praeda* here is a *nomen actionis*. Compare also Sallust's *igni magis quam praeda ager vastabatur* (*Jug.* 55.5). But *praeda* was concretized quite early in the function of a patient, 'that which is taken' → 'booty'.[14]

The pre-form of *praeda* is often given as $*pra\underline{i}\text{-}hed\bar{a}$.[15] A spelling PRAIDAD is attested early (*CIL* 1.49) and, although Leumann-Hofmann (§ 132) speak of the process as contraction, it appears that $*pra\underline{i}d\bar{a}$ resulted from the syncopation of the vowel of the root. This is apparently the same syncope that produced *praebēre* < $*pra\underline{i}\text{-}hab\text{-}\bar{e}\text{-}$.[16] It may also be noted that an -*h*- left before a consonant after syncope seems to be simply lost, thus *praeda* < $*pra\underline{i}d\bar{a}$ < $*pra\underline{i}hd\bar{a}$ < $*pra\underline{i}\text{-}h\overline{V}d\text{-}\bar{a}$. Similar cases, although without an -*h*- intervening between the preverb/preposition and the syncopated vowel, are *praetor* (PRAITOR) < $*pra\underline{i}\text{-}i\text{-}tor$ and *praemium* <

*praɩ̯-em-iɩ̯o-. If such a process is responsible for *praeda*, then it is impossible to determine exactly what the syncopated vowel was.

Secondly, this would be a type of compound (a preverb/preposition plus a verbal noun in plain -*ā*) almost unparalleled in Latin. At best, Latin normally forms compounds with the semantics of a patient by adding the suffix *-iɩ̯o-* to the preverb/preposition and verbal root. This is the type of *praemium* < *praɩ̯-em-iɩ̯o-* (*emō*) and *adāgium* < *ad-āg-iɩ̯o-*[17] (*aiō*).

Upon examining the evidence of other older IE languages, we find that Greek and Sanskrit do have compounds of a preverb/preposition plus a verbal noun in -*ā* that function as verbal nouns. But the scarcity of such formations in Homer, and their apparent absence from Vedic, suggests that this sort of compound is not inherited. How, then, would something like *praeda* have been created in Latin?

One way to answer this question is to compare how Greek seems to have done the same thing. Homer seems to have no instance of such a compound with *e*-grade of the root,[18] but we find the following examples with *o*-grade:

ἀντολαί

ἐπαοιδή

προδοκή

προχοή

συνοχή

Beside ἐπαοιδή and προχοή, the simplex forms ἀοιδή and χοή are also attested in Homer. These latter are verbal nouns of the well-known τομή-type, with *o*-grade of the root and the suffix -*ā*. Therefore, it seems reasonable to think that χοή, for example, has played some part in the creation of προχοή. The fact that both χέω and προχέω are found in Homer suggests one, although not the only, possible explanation of the προχοή-type. As is well-known, preverbs are not always attached to their verbs in Homer and hence univerbation is clearly not very old. But once the univerbation took place, the model of χοή beside χέω could easily prompt the creation of προχοή beside προχέω. So it makes sense that Vedic, which shows almost no univerbation of preverbs and verbs, also has no nominal forms like προχοή.

Given that *praɩ̯-hedā* is not an inherited type of compound, the *e*-grade cannot be established on that basis. Furthermore, no simplex **hedā* is attested and there seems to be no evidence that *e*-grade verbal nouns of this type existed in Latin. In short, there is no clear reason to think that the vowel in question was *-*e*- at all.

Latin does, however, preserve several clear examples of the τομή-type of verbal noun, e.g.,

toga : *tegō*

rota : OIr. *rethid* 'runs'

mola : OIr. *melid* 'grinds'[19]

These are residual and heavily concretized, but they do show that Latin may once have had a verbal noun of this type from the root **gʰed-*. It is true that no independent *hodā exists, but, unlike *hedā, this would at least be of a known inherited type represented in Latin. If Latin formed compounds parallel to the Greek προχοή-type, we might expect a pre-form **prai̯-hodā*. Therefore, it seems more likely that the syncopated vowel of *praeda* was an *-*o*-, rather than an *-*e*-.

If we look for other examples of the *praeda*-type of compound in Latin, we find that there are very few candidates with reasonably sure etymologies. Perhaps the best example is *ap(p)lūda* 'chaff' (Naev.+), which is almost certainly to be connected with the verb *plaudō*.[20] The preverb is most likely to be *at*, which, like *abs-*, denotes origin and/or separation. This preverb/adverb is only marginally preserved in Latin. As a preverb, it appears in *atavus* 'great-great-great-grandfather'[21], which can be straightforwardly explained as a possessive compound meaning 'having a grandfather (descended) from (him)'.[22] In a more purely adverbial usage, *at* 'but'[23] (< *ati) can be understood as having developed, from the more separative meaning of the preverb, along the same semantic lines as *sed* 'but', which contains the preverb/preposition *sĕ-* of *sēcēdō* 'go apart', *sēcūrus* 'free from care', etc.[24] Therefore, *at-* would give the right sense of separation or dispersal for *ap(p)lūda* and would no doubt assimilate to give *app-* in this position.[25]

Remora (Pl.+) 'delay' is descriptively a compound of this type, but cannot be very old since the internal short vowel has escaped reduction. *Remora* could easily have been created relatively recently by the simple analogy, *moror* : *mora* : : *remoror* : X = *remora*. This analogy would be parallel to the one proposed creating προχοή beside προχέω on the model of χοή beside χέω. It seems highly likely, therefore, that **prai̯-hodā* was made, directly or indirectly, from a *hodā also of the τομή-type.

To return to *pre(he)ndō*, one might have expected the same phonology that produced *praeda* < **prai̯-hodā* to have operated on the verb as well. Why, then, is it *pre(he)nd-*, rather than **prai̯nd-* < **prai̯-hend-*? *Prehend-* is standardly said to show that the diphthong of *$prai̯$- has become a monophthong, which was then shortened before the vowel giving $prĕ$-; and $prend$- is explained as a contraction of $prehend$-.[26] There are examples of such short scansions of -ae- in hiatus; Leumann-Hofmann (§ 118) list the following examples:

praeut (often in Pl.)

praeustīs (Verg. *Aen.* 7.524)

Pellaeō (Pl. *As.* 333 vs. 397)

Lindsay also cites *praeolat* with a short -ae- (Pl. *Mil.* 41).[27] It is notable, however, that these are sporadic instances, and thus not truly comparable to *prehendō*, in which the *pre-* never seems to be scanned as a long syllable. In addition, the occasional shortening of -ae- in *praeustīs*, etc., has apparently had no effect on the spelling, whereas *prehendō* is not usually spelled *prae-*.[28]

There is some evidence to suggest that *$prai̯$-hend- was, in fact, syncopated to *$prai̯nd$-, as the comparison with *praeda* would suggest, and that *pre(he)nd-* is secondary. Festus (p. 166 M) gives the gloss: *Nancitor in XII nactus erit, praenderit.* Notice that *praenderit* is not the strange form that Festus is explaining; it is one of the two ways he glosses the archaic *nancitor*. Of course, Festus is not an archaic author himself and so one might well hesitate to attribute such antiquity to a word found only in Festus' active vocabulary. On the other hand, he was certainly an antiquarian familiar with all sorts of linguistic archaisms and oddities, so it may well be that he picked up *praendō* from some considerably older source no longer extant.

If Festus' *praendō* preserves what might be expected, on the basis of *praeda*, to be the phonologically regular outcome of *$prai̯$-hend-, *pre(he)ndō* still remains to be explained. In attested Latin, further combinations of *pre(he)ndō* with an additional preverb, such as *appre(he)ndō*, *compre(he)ndō*, *dēpre(he)ndō*, and *repre(he)ndō*, are very common. If we assume for the moment that *$prai̯$-hend- had gone to *$prai̯nd$-, what would happen when another preverb was added? In a form such as *kom-$prai̯nd$-, the diphthong *-$ai̯$- finds itself in an internal syllable; and there is an apparent sound law in Latin by which *-$ai̯$- becomes *-$ē$- in an internal syllable before a nasal consonant.[29] The clearest example is perhaps *obscēnus* < *-$skai̯$-no-, with the root of *scaevus* and Gk. σκαι(ϝ)ός. Without this sound law, moreover, there is no obvious explanation of *aliēnus*.[30] With it, however, it is possible to hypothesize that *aliēnus* is a derivative in *-no- of the locative *$aliai̯$ of the *ā*-stem *alia* (cf., on the one hand, the *ā*-stem genitive singular *aliās* in adverbial function and, on the other, e.g., loc. πέρυσι : adj. περυσινός and gen. sg. ντcτ : adj. ντcτnus).[31]

By this rule, then, *kom-praind- would become *kom-prēnd-. From this and the other compounds, a new simplex *prēnd- could have been extracted, which would account, more or less directly, for the shorter form prendō. The only other intervening change would be the shortening of the *-ē- of *prēnd- by a relatively recent application of Osthoff's Law, which shortens long vowels before a sonorant followed by another consonant.[32] Although the length of the -e- of prendō cannot, of course, be determined from the Latin, the Romance reflex (Fr. prendre) seems to require a short -ĕ-.

Since prendō cannot, therefore, be a contraction of prehendō, the longer form must still be accounted for. Quintilian (1.5.21) describes what he considers an archaic practice of spelling -ē- as -ehe- that persisted, in some cases, even to his own day:

> Inde durat ad nos usque vehementer et comprehendere et mihi, nam mehe quoque pro me apud antiquos tragoediarum praecipue scriptores in veteribus libris invenimus.[33]

If the *-ē- of *prēnd- remained long for any length of time before being shortened by the "neo"-Osthoff, there could have been the opportunity for prehend- to have been introduced as a way of spelling *prēnd-. Thus after *prēnd- was shortened to prend-, the two spellings simply remained. The disyllabic scansion of prehend- would thus have to be a later spelling pronunciation, in apparently the same way that vēmens and vehemens are both attested.

In summary, praeda is the outcome of a syncopated *prai̯-hodā, rather than *prai̯-hedā. This *prai̯-hodā was, in all likelihood, made from a verbal abstract *hodā of the same type as Lat. toga, etc. Syncope also operated on the verbal compound, giving *prai̯nd- (cf. Fest. praenderit) from *prai̯-hend-. When an additional preverb was added, *-prai̯nd- became *-prēnd- by an apparently regular Latin sound change, by which *-ai̯- becomes *-ē- in an internal syllable before a nasal consonant. From such compounds as *kom-prēnd-, etc., a new simplex *prēnd- was extracted and this form, with what seems to be an archaic spelling of -ē- as -ehe-, is probably preserved in prehendō. The by-form prendō, on the other hand, would seem to represent the phonologically regular outcome of *prēnd- after the -ē- underwent an Osthoff-type shortening.

NOTES

1. For this root etymology, see W-H, E-M, etc.
2. Lindsay, *Early Latin Verse* (Oxford, 1922), p. 151.
3. Thurneysen, *KZ* 63 (1936) p. 115.

4. The semantics of the Germanic verbs are comparable to Lat. *incipiō*, that is, 'take on, up' → 'begin'.
5. This is an unusual root shape to make a nasal infix present, but compare *b^heg*- which makes Skt. *bhanakti* 'breaks'.
6. Such analogical spreading of a present-forming nasal infix throughout a paradigm is common in Latin, cf. *iungō, iunxī, iunctus* (but nominal *iugum*) vs. Skt. pres. *yunakti*, aor. *ayujat*, perf. *yuyoja*, ppl. *yukta-*.
7. It is very difficult to see how this isolated *e*-grade could be an innovation; it is much more likely to be a relic of an older state of affairs.
8. See above, note 3.
9. G. Meyer, *Etymologisches Wörterbuch der Albanesischen Sprache*.
10. Rix, p. 211.
11. Klingenschmitt, *Das Altarmenische Verbum*, p. 164 ff.
12. The following scenario describing the history of the Armenian *-an-$^e/_o$-presents and the role of χανδάνω in the creation of the Greek double-nasal presents was outlined to me by J. Jasanoff in a personal communication.
13. *OLD* 1c. Note, however, that in the passage of Accius (*tr.* 271 W: *passimque praedam pecua vallebant agris*) given under this heading, *praeda*, especially since it appears to be in apposition to *pecua*, could well mean simply 'booty'. Thus I would translate, 'and on all sides they walled in the flocks taken as booty'.
14. *OLD* 1a (*CIL* 1.25+), from which 'potential booty' (1b), 'prey' (2), and 'reward, prize, profit' (3) are reasonable developments.
15. Pokorny, L-H § 132, Bader § 102, etc.
16. *Praehibēre* is almost certainly recompounded from the preverb and existing simplex *habēre* and the scansion of *praehib*- is ambiguous between ˘ ˘ and — —. Also, *praebia* 'prophylactic amulets' may be from *$prai$-hab-iio-, but the etymology is not entirely clear.
17. The long -*ā*- here must be analogical, as it is in other members of this morphological category, such as *contāgium*, and in similar formations, such as *ambāgēs* and *compāgēs*.
18. The source of the following information on Homeric nominal formations is Risch.
19. *Mola* is reconstructed with an *o*-grade for morphological reasons, although **mel*- or **mol*- would ultimately give *mol*- in Latin. Hence, *molō* is likewise ambiguous and could go back to an *e*-grade (cf. OIr. *melid*) or an *o*-grade (cf. Go. *malan*).
20. E-M simply dismiss the word as non-Roman. W-H, on the other hand, connect *applūda* with the verb *plaudō* and the preverb/preposition is generally assumed to be *abs-*. Although a concretization of *abs-$ploud$-$ā$ with a passive meaning, like *praeda*, would give a good description of chaff as 'that which is beaten away', this pre-form raises a phonological problem. The regular outcome of *$abs + p$- is *as-*, as in *asportō* 'carry away' and *aspellō* 'drive away'. A variant spelling *adplūda* is, in fact, attested in Pliny (*Nat. Hist.* 18.99.6) and if the preverb/preposition of *ap(p)lūda* were *ad-*, the phonology would work, but the semantics would be less than satisfactory.
21. W-H connect *atavus* with**at(i)*. E-M, on the other hand, accept the etymology of Festus: *at[t]avus, quia atta est avi, id est pater* .... But if an *atavus* is to be understood as the father of an *avus*, he would only be a great-grandfather.
22. As such, *atavus* is entirely parallel to, although more archaic than, *abavus* 'great-great-grandfather'.

23. Also found as the first part of *atque, atquī*. Among the cognates are the first parts of Gk. ἀτ-αρ 'but' and Go. *appan* ' ἀλλὰ υοῦν' (E-M, W-H) as well as OIr. *aith-* '*re-, ex-*' (W-H, Thurneysen, p. 500).
24. As a sort of postposition, *-at* has contracted, apparently with the stem vowel, to give the inherited *o*-stem ablative singular in *-ōd* (Lat. GNAIVOD, Skt. *devā̆t*, Lith. *dievo*, etc.) < *-o-at*. For a more detailed discussion, see Stang, *Vergleichende Grammatik der Baltischen Sprachen*.
25. Pliny's *adp-* is probably secondarily extracted from *app-* (W-H), since most cases of surface *app-* were easily analyzable as *ad + p-*, whereas *at-* was no longer a synchronically recognizable preverb/preposition.
26. L-H, § 118, 133; Lindsay, *op. cit.* p. 151.
27. *Op. cit.*, p. 151
28. The spelling *praehend-* is found, but apparently only consistently in Justinian and the *Scriptores Historiae Augustae*, where it has probably been reconstituted.
29. I am indebted to A. Nussbaum for suggesting the possibility of this sound law.
30. L-H (§ 294.2.b) follow the suggestion of Skutsch (*Glotta* 3, p. 355) that *aliēnus* is dissimilated from *ali-īno-*, but the only parallel given is *laniēna* (*taberna*) 'butcher's shop'. But the etymology of this word is unclear and the putative derivational morphology, *-i̯o-* (*lanius*) : *-i-īno-* (→ *laniēnus*), is highly questionable in view of *Latium* : *Latīnus*, etc.
31. *Terrēnus* could also be derived from the locative of the *ā*-stem, *terra*, but is usually taken to be from the neuter *s*-stem (OIr. *tír* 'land') with *-ēno-* from *-es-no-* (cf. *aēnus* 'brazen' with *aes* 'bronze'). See L-H, § 294.2.
32. cf. *ŭndecim* (Fr. *onze*) < *ūnidecim* < *oi̯no-*.
33. The inclusion of *mihi* (cf. Umbr. *mehe*) here is misleading, since it is actually older than *mī*, which is contracted from it.

20
opēs, opitulā

tr. 20–22 W: *Da mihi*
     hasce opes quas peto, quas precor! Porrige,
     opitula!

The etymological dictionaries[1] standardly connect *ops* with a large assortment of words, both within Latin and without, whose relationships may now be clarified on the basis of recent work in the phonology of the Anatolian languages.

One meaning of *ops*, 'wealth, resource', accords well with a derivational family in Hittite, consisting of the denominative verbs *ḫappinaḫḫ-* 'enrich' and *ḫappineš-* 'become rich' and the adjectives *ḫappina-*, *ḫappinant-* 'rich'. That this family is related to *ops*, I do not believe has ever been denied. The same may be said of Skt. *apnas-* 'wealth' and Av. *afnahvant-* 'wealthy'. Slightly removed semantically, but almost certainly to be associated with these, are Hitt. neut. nom.-acc. sg. *ḫappir, ḫappar* 'business, trade; compensation, price', *ḫapparai-* 'trade, sell', *ḫappir(iy)a-* 'city, town' (as the center of commerce; the original meaning was probably 'marketplace'), Lycian *epirijeti* 'sells', etc.

The Hittite evidence shows that the root had an initial laryngeal, either $*h_2$- or $*h_3$- ($*h_1$- being lost in all positions in Hittite). Therefore, Lat. *op-* could go back to $*h_2op$-, $*h_3ep$-, or $*h_3op$-. Although Hittite is of no help in determining which of the two laryngeals is correct in this position, Lyc. *epirijeti* with an initial vowel shows that the laryngeal in question must have been $*h_3$-, since an initial $*h_2$- remains in Lycian, e.g. *xñtawa-* 'rule' with Hitt. *ḫant-* 'front' $< *h_2ent$-.[2]

So we are left with a choice between $*h_3ep$- or $*h_3op$- for Lat. *op-*. Of course, $*h_3ep$- would have been colored to $*h_3op$- already in the proto-language, but the original nominative singular is attested as *ops* in Accius, (*Inc.* 5 W),[3] and in the divine name *Ops (Consiva)*.[4] Therefore we are dealing with a feminine root noun verbal abstract, originally meaning 'abundance', from a verbal root meaning 'to abound'. In such a noun from a root of this shape we would expect *e/z*-ablaut (cf. *nex*), so *ops* is more likely to reflect $*h_3op$-*s* from, in the last analysis, $*h_3ep$-*s*.[5]

The other cognates would then be reconstructed as follows: Skt. *apnas-* would go back to $*h_3ep$-*no-s-* or $*h_3op$-*no-s-*.[6] The same *s*-stem with the IE possessive suffix *-u̯ent-* underlies Av. *afnahvant-*. Hitt. *ḫappina-* is the reflex of this denominative adjective in *-no-* and goes back to $*h_3ep$-*en-o-*, which is in turn derived from an *r/n*-stem substantive (cf. Skt. *tapana-* $< *tep$-*eno-*). As often in Hittite, the adjective

57

received an -*nt*-extension, giving *ḫappinant*-. Hitt. *ḫappír* is from *$*h_3p\text{-}ér$.[7] Finally, *ḫappar(iy)a*- looks to be from *$*h_3p\text{-}er\text{-}o\text{-}$.

The handbooks almost universally connect this derivational family with Lat. *opus* and a group of apparently cognate words with meanings related to 'effort' or 'work', particularly of a ritual nature. But the reconstruction of the root *$*h_3ep\text{-}$ for *ops* effectively rules out the possibility of such a connection. While *opus* itself phonologically could be from *$*h_3ep\text{-}e/os\text{-}$, it has been suggested that *opus* should be from the same root as *epula(e)/-um* 'banquet', which seems to have originally meant 'a religious work or performance',[8] a meaning which was later specialized to mean 'a sacrificial meal', then '(public) feast, banquet'. If, therefore, *opus* and *epula(e)/-um* are derived from the same root, this root cannot be *$*h_3ep\text{-}$ because this would have become *$*h_3op\text{-}$ already in the proto-language and *epula(e)/-um* , with its initial *e-*, could never have come from this. The root of this family would therefore have to be set up as *$*h_1ep\text{-}$, *$*h_1\text{-}$ being the only laryngeal which would not color a following short -*ĕ*-. *Epula/epulum* would ultimately be an instrumental noun in -*la/-lum* (cf. *rēgula*, *strāgulum*) with anaptyxis.[9] *Opus* itself would, in that case, go back to *$*h_1op\text{-}$ with *o*-grade of the root. Although a root *e*-grade is expected in neuter *s*-stems, it is a fact that Latin has several *o*-grade *s*-stems, e.g. *pondus*, *foedus*, *mūnus*. Also to be taken with this root are Skt. *ápas*- 'work' < *$*h_1e/op\text{-}os\text{-}$, Ved. *ápas*- 'cult-act' < *$*h_1ē/ōp\text{-}os\text{-}$ and *āpra*- 'sacrificer' < *$*h_1ē/ōp\text{-}ro\text{-}$, and OHG *uoben* 'to celebrate a festival' and *uoba* 'festival' < *$*h_1ōp\text{-}$. Since the root shapes are demonstrably different, none of these words can be related to *ops*.

Opitulo(r)[10] clearly contains the stem of *ops* and is most simply interpreted as a denominative from the adjective *opitulus*, which is attested as a cult-title of Jupiter in Paul. *Fest.* (p. 184 M.).[11] *Opitulus* itself would seem to be a compound, of the same type as *foedifragus*, from the root *$*telh_2\text{-}$ without, of course, the nasal infix of the present *tollō* < *$*tḷ\text{-}n\text{-}h_2\text{-}$.

The question of whether Lat. *ops* and *opus* are etymologically related can now, perhaps, be settled, with the application of discoveries made in the area of Anatolian phonology. The semantics of *ops* strongly suggest a connection with Hitt. *ḫappina*-, etc., which means that this family must be reconstructed with an initial *$*h_2\text{-}$ or *$*h_3\text{-}$. But this semantic group also includes Lyc. *epirijeti*, which can only have had an initial *$*h_3\text{-}$. *Ops* and its cognates, therefore, must go back to a root *$*h_3ep\text{-}$.

On the other hand, Lat. *opus* belongs to a family of words with semantics suggesting 'work', often of a religious sort. Most of these words (e.g., *opus*, Skt. *ápas*-) are also compatible with *$*h_3ep\text{-}$. But since it is very likely that Lat. *epula(e)/ epulum* is etymologically connected with *opus*, this family must have had an initial *$*h_1\text{-}$. Lat. *ops* and *opus* must, in that case, be etymologically unrelated and go back to two distinct roots *$*h_3ep\text{-}$ and *$*h_1ep\text{-}$, respectively.

NOTES

1. See, for example, Pokorny or W-H, but also such recent works as Tischler's *Hethitiches etymologisches Glossar* (Innsbruck, 1977–).
2. S. Kimball, "*H_3 in Anatolian" *Festschrift Hoenigswald*, p. 185–92 (although Kimball considers both Lat. *ops* and *opus* to be from *h_3ep-). See also now Melchert, p. 72.
3. Priscian (*ap. G.L.* II.321.24), cites this fragment (*quorum genitor fertur esse ops gentibus*) saying that *ops* is an adjective used by archaic writers to mean *opulentus*, but here has the meaning "*opem ferens et auxilium*". The fact that in this passage *ops* does not have what Priscian gives as the usual meaning seems to indicate that he has confused an example of the root noun with an adjective *ops* also attested in Paul. *Fest.* (p. 191 M: *Ops antiqui dicebant opulentum, unde e contrario inops*). This adjective is probably to be explained as a back-formation from *inops*.
4. Varro, *LL* 5.57. The nom. sg. also appears as *Opis* (Pl. *Bac.* 893, Hyg. *Fab.* 139.1, Paul. *Fest.*, p. 187 M), but this has been remade in the same way as *frūgis* from *frux* and *vehis* from **vex*.
5. J. Schindler "L'apophonie des noms-racines Indo-Européens" *BSL* 67, p. 37 f.
6. A neuter adjectival abstract in -*s*- can be derived from a thematic adjective, cf. Gk. πῆρος, -εος 'diability' from πηρός 'disabled'.
7. Its expected locative *ḫappíri* < *h_3p-ér+i is attested, but also a locative *ḫappari*, which appears to be remade analogically on the basis of the stem of the other oblique forms, *h_3p-(r)r-.
8. See E-M for this meaning of *epula(e)/-um*.
9. See L-H, § 283.
10. Note that this fragment of Livius is the only place where the active inflection is attested.
11. Bader, § 97.

29
praestōlārās

tr. 29 W: *Nimis pol inprudenter servus praestolaras.*

Nonius (p. 475 L) cites this fragment to illustrate the active inflection of the verb *praestōlo(r)* as opposed to the deponent inflection regular in classical Latin and found as early as Plautus and Terence. But a non-deponent form is also attested in Turpilius *Com.* 153. This issue of deponent versus non-deponent inflection has been used as evidence in the larger and much-debated question, to which we shall now turn, of the morphology and etymology of *praestōlo(r)*.

In spite of these early active forms, Stowasser suggests that the deponent inflection is original on the basis of his analysis of the verb as a back-formation from an expression *praestōlātus*, meaning 'having brought oneself [so as to be] at hand (*praestō*)'.[1] Stowasser detects an element of motion in the meaning of the adverb *praestō* on the evidence of a passage of Tibullus which he gives as "*tibi praestō pauper adibit*" (1.5.61). From this he argues that the adverb could have been paired with other verbs of motion, including *ferō* used in the (medio-)passive.[2]

The argument would be somewhat stronger if there were an example of the phrase (*praestō ferrī*) whose perfect (*praestō lātus*) is the alleged starting point for the back-formation. Nevertheless, if this scenario were correct, one might expect the perfect participial forms of *praestōlo(r)* to be attested in early texts more frequently than the present stem, but this is not the case.[3]

There are also phonological problems with the idea of a univerbation of *praestō* and *lātus*. The combination should be reasonably old, given the extreme scarcity of the participial forms to which *praestōlo(r)* is said to have been back-formed. Its antiquity is also implied by the necessary assumption that the present *praestōlo(r)* has been created and is so well entrenched that there is no longer any trace of an expression *praestō ferō*. For all this to have already taken place, the univerbation should probably have occurred at a time when the forms involved were *praestō* (or *praestōd*[4]) and **tlātus* (< **tḷh₂-to-*). If so, the initial *tl-* of **tlātus* would have been in a word-internal position and should have given, at first, **-kl-* (cf. *pōc(u)lum* 'drinking-vessel' < **pōklo-* < **pō-tlo-*). Of course, if the original univerbation were still transparent enough after *tlātus* had become *lātus*, it would have been a simple matter to remake the univerbation on the analogy of the free-standing form. But if the component parts of the univerbation could still be identified in order to remake *praestōlātus* (instead of **praestōc(u)lātus*), they cannot at the same time have been so opaque as to generate a new present *praestōlo(r)*.

Perhaps even more damaging to this theory is the fact that the Tibullus passage does not really offer any proof of the use of *praestō* with a verb of motion. Stowasser's presentation is rather misleading. The passage, according to the 1988 Teubner edition by G. Luck, reads:

> *Pauper erit praesto semper tibi, pauper adibit*
> *primus et in tenero fixus erit latere,*

Although the text is problematic at this point, most editors (e.g., Luck, Putnam, Smith, Postgate) punctuate the line with either a comma or a colon before the second *pauper*. The balance of the phrases certainly seems to require that *praestō* be taken with the preceding verb.[5] Furthermore, even if *praestōlātus* came to be univerbated, it must have still been construed as a past participle. Therefore, the present of a verb back-formed from this would have to mean 'bring oneself [so as to be] *praestō*', while *praestolo(r)* seems to mean simply 'be *praestō*'.[6]

In short, this theory encounters obstacles at every stage. Although *ferō* is extremely common, it is apparently never found with *praestō*. The participial forms from which *praestōlor* is said to have been formed, are virtually non-existent in older Latin. Thus there does not seem to have been sufficient time to completely lose these traces of the history of a univerbated *praestōlātus* that was formed (or analogically re-formed) recently enough to show simple *lātus*, rather than **tlātus* or some development thereof.

If *praestōlo(r)* originally meant 'be *praestō*', Stowasser's idea of a derivation from the adverb is attractive in this respect at least. The difficulty, of course, is to account for the *-l-* of the stem. Some scholars have tried to solve the problem by denying the connection with *praestō* (adv.) entirely and proposing a root with a final *-l-*.

Bréal,[7] following a suggestion of Meillet,[8] argues that *praestōlo(r)* is from the root **stel-* 'to place', although, unlike Meillet, he may have believed that the medial *-o-* of *praestōlo(r)* is short.[9] Bréal tries to support this etymology on semantic grounds by comparing the use of στόλος '(sea-)voyage; expedition; fleet' and στέλλω 'rig out (a ship); (med-pass.) set out' in nautical contexts, and therefore proposes that *praestōlo(r)* properly means 'wait on dry land (for a ship)'.[10] There are two problems with this theory. Firstly, the long *-ō-* of *praestōlo(r)* is guaranteed at Plautus *Epid.* 221 at least. Secondly, the passages said to show that the verb could be used of people awaiting ships are neither so numerous nor so early as to be convincing examples of the original meaning of the word. The instance from Terence is especially puzzling since Parmeno has just encountered his master returning from the country to town; it is not clear that any boat is involved.

Since all attempts so far to find a root in final *-l-* for *praestōlo(r)* have been unsatisfactory, and since no objection can be made to the semantic appropriateness of a derivation from *praestō*, it would seem best to begin from the adverb. First, however, it will be useful to consider the morphology of *praestō* (adv.) itself.

Solmsen (*Glotta* 3, p. 245 ff.) suggests that *praestō* is the nominative singular of an *ōn*-stem, meaning 'one who stands before', that has become isolated.[11] From this a denominative verb *praestōnā- 'to be one who stands before' (→ 'to await') was formed, cf. *caupō* 'tradesman' : *caupōnā*- 'to engage in trade'. This *praestōnā- then underwent a dissimilation of -*t*- . . . -*n*- to -*t*- . . . -*l*-, giving *praestōlo(r)*. To grant the first premise of this theory, that *praestō* (adv.) is a fossilized substantive, one would have to accept that the rest of the paradigm was lost, but this is not a major obstacle; the same sort of thing must have happened according to almost any explanation of the adverb. The real difficulty emerges in the final stage, the dissimilation of -*n*- to -*l*-. No reasonably plausible parallels for such a development have been identified in Latin.

A better explanation of *praestō* (adv. > It. *presto* 'soon, quickly') is suggested by the discussions of Prellwitz[12] and Persson.[13] The adverb would appear to be either the instrumental or ablative singular of a compound going back to **prai̯-sth₂-o-*, the second member being the zero-grade of the root of *stō*, and therefore meaning, in the first instance, 'standing before' or the like. Such a compound would give a Latin adjective *praestus* (> Fr. *prêt* 'ready'), and this is attested (*CIL* 6.12013.11), but may well be a back-formation from *praestō* (adv.) itself.[14] Even if the attested adjective is not directly inherited, it must have recreated what had already existed, since the adjective is required to explain the adverb *praestō*.[15]

This analysis of *praestō* (adv.) is not entirely without problems either. If it is the instrumental or ablative of an *o*-stem, the -*ō* should be old. But Cassiodorus the grammarian remarks: *praesto nos per o scribimus, veteres per u scripserunt, sed sic praesto dicendum est ut sedulo* (VII.157.22). The form *praestu* is even attested in inscriptions (*CIL* 6.4416; 6.37763 a & b), although apparently not from an early date, the first instance being dated probably to the Augustan period. If *praestū*, presumably with a long -*ū*, is actually the original form of the adverb, it is probably from a *u*-stem substantive derived from the *o*-stem adjective, standing to *praestus* in the same relationship as *promptū* to *promptus*. But this suggests another explanation for *praestū*, namely that, since *praestō* and *promptū* are so similar in meaning, it is conceivable that *praestō* was remade to *praestū* under the influence of *promptū*.[16] In any case, there is no reason to believe that *praestū* is the earlier form of the adverb.

H. Ehrlich, however, dismisses Persson's theory of *praestō* (adv.) as unsatisfactory, because it fails to take into account the formation of *praestōlo(r)*.[17] Ehrlich begins his own explanation of the verb by declaring his belief, on the basis of the Cassiodorus passage, that *praestū* is the older form of the adverb[18] and goes on to deny that the adverb *praestō* is in any way connected with the verb(s) *praestō*. From the fact that the adverb means virtually the same as *praesens*, Erhlich argues that *prae-s-tū*, as he divides it, is the ablative of a verbal noun, of the type of *portus* and *transitus*, made from the weak stem of the root **h₁es-* 'to be'. To this he compares the Hesychius gloss ἀπ-εστύς 'absence'. *Praestōlo(r)*, Ehrlich suggests, comes from a **prae-stŏ[u̯]-lo-*, which he proposes is a proto-Italic derivative of the stem of *prae-s-tu*.

Ehrlich's pre-form **prae-stŏ[u̯]-lo-* is both phonologically and morphologically difficult. The brackets around the **-u̯-* seem to mean that the glide disappeared when the **-lo-* suffix was added. While this treatment of a **-u̯l-* cluster is not inconceivable, there seems to be no source for the preceding -ŏ- in a derivative of a *tu*-stem. Also, one might rather expect that the **-ŏu̯-* would have been treated as a diphthong and come out eventually as -ū-. Also, the morphological analysis of the -*lo*- suffix is unclear. It would appear that **prae-stŏ[u̯]-lo-* is meant to be a diminutive in **-lo-*. But Latin seems not to have any derivatives of this type from *tu*-stems. In short, the idea of a *tu*-stem seems altogether unlikely here and Ehrlich's arguments do nothing to confirm that *praestū* is older than *praestō*. Therefore, there is no reason to dismiss the idea that *praestō* is from an *o*-stem paradigm.

Although Persson does not attempt to explain the morphology of *praestōlo(r)*, there are at least two ways in which the verb could have been formed from an original *praestō* with the sort of history he proposes. First, if the adverb is an ablative, the inherited ending would have been **-ōd*. From this **prai̯stōd*, a first conjugation verb could be derived in the same way as *autumāre* and *negāre* are derived from the adverbs *autem* and *nec* respectively. The -*d*- in this **prai̯stōd-ā-* could then have undergone a change to -*l*-.[19] This would be the so-called "Sabine -*l*-" also used to explain *lingua* (vs. Old Latin *dingua* and Gmc. **tungōn-*), *lēvir* (vs. Gk. δαήρ and Skt. *devar-*), *oleō* (vs. *odor*), etc. It is dangerous, however, to start from a **prai̯stōd*, since the adverb seems never to be attested with a final -*d*, nor does it occur in hiatus with any noticeable frequency, if ever, in early Latin.

But another explanation is possible that does not require *praestō* to be an old ablative. If a morphological boundary cannot be placed just after the -*l*-, then perhaps one can be placed before it. Ernout-Meillet propose, with a query, that *praestōlo(r)* may be a denominative verb from a **praestō-lo-*. Although they do not make it explicit, this pre-form is presumably meant to be a diminutive in -*lo*- from *praestō* (adv.). While diminutive forms of adverbs are known, e.g., *clanculum* (*clam*), no such form from *praestō* is actually attested.

We have already observed that Latin is capable of deriving verbs from adverbs (*autumāre*, *negāre*) by simply adding -*ā*- as the stem vowel. If one wanted to create such a verb from *praestō*, there would be a problem with the -*ā*- contracting with the final vowel of the adverb[20] and the result would probably be another verb *praestō* to add to the confusion of the other two. Latin can, however, form denominative verbs with the suffix -(e)*lā*-, as well as with simple -*ā*-, e.g., *violāre* beside *vīs*, for which there is no diminutive substantive attested.[21] And although the -(e)*l*- of this formant is very probably to be traced to the inherited suffix *-e-lo-*, which derives endocentric substantives from substantives, such a diminutive substantive is by no means a prerequisite for the creation of a denominative verb in *-lā-*. Therefore the verbal suffix *-lā-* would be a convenient way of avoiding this problem and keeping the adverbial basis separate from the verbal morphology.

Another possible explanation of *praestōlo(r)* is suggested by the fact that although in most cases *praestōlo(r)* does seem simply to mean 'wait for' with no movement on the part of the subject indicated, there is at least one example in early Latin in which the verb would better be translated 'go to meet'. In Plautus' *Epidicus*, the title character comments on the great number of *meretices* in the city who are running to meet (*obviam occurebant*) their lovers and describes how he has seen one particular woman: *atque ego illam illi video praestolarier | et cum ea tibicinae ibant quattuor* (217 f.). If four flute-players were going (*ībant*) along with this woman, she is unlikely to have been standing still waiting. This raises the possiblity that *praestōlo(r)* contains a verb of motion.

Latin preserves a likely candidate in *pālor* 'wander' (< *pe-al-*) and *ambulō* 'walk' (< *amb(i)-al-*), both compounds of a root *h_2el-* also found in Gk. ἀλάομαι 'wander'.[22] *Praestōlo(r)* would then have to be explained as a univerbation of this verb **alō* and a form *praestō* meaning not 'at hand, at the ready', but rather 'to hand, to the ready'. The semantics in that case would seem to require a directive case form.

Remains of the inherited directive are few in Latin and mostly from pronominal stems, e.g., *adeō* 'to this point' and *quoad* 'to what point', whose function is clear from the univerbation with *ad*. But it is difficult to know whether the original directive of the *o*-stem adjective *praestus* would have been *praestō*. There is comparative evidence, however, to suggest that the inherited thematic directive in *-o-h_2e* gave *-oh_2* then *-ō* (> Hitt. -*a*), which would give -*ō* in Latin.[23]

Nevertheless, it is not necessary to claim that *praestō* really preserves the original directive morphology. There was apparently a synchronic process in Latin by which functional directives were created by simply dropping the final *-d* from the corresponding ablative singular form; this is needed to account for expressions like *meā rē fert* 'it concerns me'. This process could easily have been suggested by pattern of the original directive *quō* 'whither' beside the ablative *quōd*. Thus, from the ablative of a substantivized neuter of *praesto-*, meaning 'readiness' or the like, a new directive *praestō* 'to the ready' could be formed.

If *praestōlo(r)* does contain a directive and originally meant something like 'come, go to the ready', one would have to assume a slight semantic shift to 'be ready', but this would not be unnatural once the simplex **alō* was lost and *praestōlo(r)* was synchronically associated with *praestō* 'at hand'.

It seems most likely, therefore, that *praestōlo(r)* is composed of a directive *praestō*, whether this was formed with the inherited directive morphology or created later from the ablative of *$pra\underset{\,}{i}$-sth_2-o-, and a verb *alō, probably also preserved in pālor and ambulō.

NOTES

1. Das Verbum lare, p. 14.
2. For ferrī meaning 'to proceed, go', see meaning 4 under ferō in the OLD. The usage is attested as early as Pacuvius (Inc. 31 W).
3. There is but one instance of a perfect participial form in Plautus, at Truc. 336 (nescio quem praestolata est; credo militem), although even here the text is not absolutely secure. There are no such participial forms in Livius, Naevius, Ennius, Accius, Pacuvius, Caecilius, Lucilius, Cato, or Terence.
4. On the possibility that praestō (adv.) is an old abl., see below.
5. Note that this is a form of the verb 'to be', with which the adverb, appearing most commonly in the expression praestō est (often written praestost), is typically used.
6. This is essentially the definition of Festus (Praestolari is dicitur qui ante stando ibi, p. 223 M) and of Donatus (praestolari est praesto esse, on Eun. 975).
7. MSL 15, p. 141 f.
8. MSL 9, p. 15.
9. He comments "Le seul dictionnaire qui, à ma connaissance, ait bien décomposé ce mot, celui de Vaniček, marque cependant l'o du signe de la longue." (p. 142, n. 1).
10. Bréal cites Caes. B.C. II.23; Ter. Eun. 975; Cic. Att. II.15 as examples of such a meaning in Latin.
11. See also F. Skutsch, Glotta 2, p. 389 ff.
12. BB. 19, p. 318.
13. Beitr. 240 f.
14. cf. sēdulus from sēdulō (< sē dolō).
15. Either praestus or praestō is the basis of the verb praestō, -āre, -āvī 'make available, provide, offer', a factitive of the (re-)novāre-type that has become confused with praestō, -āre, -itī 'be superior', which is simply a compound of prae and stō.
16. F. Skutsch, op. cit., p. 389, n. 1.
17. Berliner Philologische Wochenschrift (1913), p. 1201 f.
18. It is worth bearing in mind that even if we believe the 'veteres' used a certain form, this is no guarantee that it is the older form. After all, Priscian (II.208.18) tells us that the 'vetustissimi' used the form carnis as nominative singular, as in Livius Od. 45 W, instead of carō, which is clearly the inherited form. Not all innovations, however early the date, catch on.
19. See W-H under praestōlo(r).
20. If the adverb is an old ablative, one would have to assume that the verb was created only after the final -d was lost.
21. For a more detailed discussion, see the appendix. It is also possible that violāre was formed from the ablative vī, used as an adverb.
22. See M. Weiss, Studies in Italic Nominal Morphology, Cornell University dissertation (1993), p. 53.
23. Melchert, p. 51, with reference to Jasanoff.

38
nefrendem, lacteam inmulgens opem

tr. 38 W: *quem ego nefrendem alui lacteam inmulgens opem*

Nefrendem is the accusative singular of an adjective whose nominative is unattested, but generally agreed to be *nefrens* < *ne-frend-s. The word otherwise only occurs in contexts where it is being defined, but in this fragment, it is used of an infant nursing and therefore the meaning 'not biting', i.e., 'toothless', reported by Festus seems appropriate (*ait Q. Mucius Scaevola esse arietes, quod dentibus frendere non possint; Ateius Capito infantes esse nondum frendentes, id est frangentes*).[1] Varro, although referring to pigs, gives a very similar definition: *amisso nomine lactantes dicuntur nefrendes ab eo, quod nondum fabam frendere possunt, id est frangere.*[2]

The infrequency of the word led to some confusion already among the ancient grammarians. Festus adds that: *sunt qui nefrendes testiculos dici putent* and *pro nefrendibus alii nefrundines intellegunt, quos usus recens dicit vel renes vel testiculos, quos Lanuvini appellant nebrundines, Graeci* νεφρούς, *Praenestini nefrones.*[3] Both of these passages point to the error made explicit in the second, namely that *nefrend-* has become confounded with *nefrundin-*.[4] It is *nefrundines* (< **neg^{uh}ro-n+d-*), which may be a dialect form, that is actually cognate with Gk. νεφρός 'kidney' and Praen. *nefrōnēs* 'kidneys'.

Nefrens would appear to be a compound, with the semantics of an agent, whose first member is the privative *nĕ-* and whose second member is a root noun from the same root as *frendĕre/frendere* 'to bite, gnash the teeth' (*$g^{uh}re(n)d$- > Gmc. **grind-* 'grind').

The difficulty, as Bader points out,[5] is that the full-grade version *nĕ-* should not appear in a true nominal compound. Apparent cases, such as *nefās* 'not right, wrong', *nescius* 'not knowing', and *nēmō* 'no one', are in reality univerbations, extracted from sentences like *ne fas est ...* 'it is not right ...', which have been reinterpreted as negative determinative compounds. Genuine compounds, on the other hand, regularly have the zero-grade form of the privative **n̥-* (> Lat. *in-*, Gk. ἀ-, Gmc. *un-*, etc.).

In this line of Livius, *infrens would scan just as well and this raises the question, why would *nefrens* have been preferable? One can only speculate, but it seems possible that *infrens might have been misconstrued as containing the preposition/preverb *in-*, and hence thought to mean 'biting (on)', cf. *infrendere*.

A comparable alternation may be observed in the pair *infans* and *nefans*. *Infans* ordinarily means 'not speaking', but is attested once in Accius with the apparent meaning 'not to be spoken (of)'.[6] *Nefans*, on the other hand, is used (twice by Lucilius[7]) only in the latter sense, synonymous with *nefandus*.

In any case, *nefrens* should not be a very old form and would appear to be analogical. Latin has very few words like *nefrens* with a stem of the shape -*Vnd*-, but one is *dēprans* (Naev.) 'not eating (= not having eaten) lunch'. Furthermore, in *dēprans*, the preposition/preverb *dē*- has essentially the same privative sense as the *ne*- of *nefrens*, cf. *dēplūmis* 'having no feathers', etc. Therefore *dēprans*, beside the verb *prandēre* 'to eat lunch', would appear to be a likely model for the creation of a compound like *nefrens* from *frendēre*.

The basis of *dēprans* itself may well have been an agent noun *prans (< *pram-ed-s) of the same structure as, for example, *praeses* (< **prai̯-sed-s*). If a reasonably old form *prans actually existed, it could provide an explanation for the verb *prandēre*, whose -*ē*- is otherwise difficult to account for, in the face of the simplex *edĕre* 'to eat'.[8] The pattern of *praeses* : *praesidium* : *praesidēre* could have prompted the creation of *prandēre* beside *prans and *prandium*.

The formation of *dēprans* is probably modeled, in turn, on compounds of the type *lībripens*, lit. 'balance-hanger', (*XII Tables*, 8.22 W), whose second member is a root noun *pens < **p(e)nd-s* (cf. *pendĕre*, *pendēre*) that also comes to have a stem ending in -*Vnd*-.

* * *

The syntax of the phrase *lacteam inmulgens opem* is somewhat surprising at first glance. The verb means to 'to milk into, to express milk into'. The thing into which the milk is expressed appears in the dative case, as *labrīs* does in the following passages:

> *hic natam in dumis interque horrentia lustra*
> *armentalis equae mammis et lacte ferino*
> *nutribat teneris inmulgens ubera labris.*   (Verg., *Aen.* 11.570–2),

> *fabulosum enim arbitror de strigibus ubera eas infantium labris*
> *immulgere.*   (Plin., *Nat.* 11.232).

But in both of these examples *ūbera* is in the accusative, whereas in the Livian fragment the milk itself, *lacteam opem*, is in that case. There seems to be no other instance in classical Latin of 'milk' as the direct object of *inmulgeō*. Only very late, starting in the fourth century AD, do we find parallels to the Livian syntax, first in Firmicus *Math.* (*nato homini ... inmulgentur alimenta nutricia*, 3.14.10) and later yet in Symmachus (*praecepta rhetoricae pectori meo senex ... inmulsit*, *epist.* 9.88.3).

In the one other place where Pliny uses *inmulgeō* the verb is passive but its subject cannot be the *ubera* one might expect from the active usage:

> ... *oculo ictu cruore suffuso et in dolore aut epiphora, si inmulgeatur, plurimum prodest,* (*Nat.* 28.72).

The passage can be translated: "[milk] is most beneficial for an eye bloodshot and painful from a blow or an inflammation, if milked into [the eye]." If 'milk' can be the subject of a passive form of *inmulgeō*, it follows that an active form of the verb could take 'milk' as an accusative object. This passage could be indirect evidence that Livius' construction *lacteam inmulgens opem* is not so anomalous.

The phrase *si inmulgeatur, plurimum prodest* is open to another interpretation, however. If *inmulgeatur* and *prodest* are being used impersonally here, rather than with *lac* as the subject, the sentence could then be translated: "it is most beneficial ... if there is milk put in." Therefore, this passage of Pliny is probably too ambiguous to be useful for these purposes.

Thus we are left with *inmulgeō* indicating an action properly performed only on *ubera*. But there are expressions in Latin in which the word for an item that is pressed is replaced by the word for the product obtained by that pressing. For example, we find phrases like "*oleum premi oportebit*" (Col. *RR* 12.52.22), literally 'the oil ought to be pressed', although of course what is actually to be pressed are the olives (*oleae* or *olivae*) from which the oil is extracted. In just such a way, Livius may be substituting *lacteam opem* (= *lac*), the result of pressing *ubera*, for the *ubera* themselves.

NOTES

1. P. 163 M.
2. *RR* 2.4.17.
3. P. 163 M; cf. p. 277 M.: *rienes quos nunc vocamus, antiqui nefrundines appellabant.*
4. See also Bader, p. 61.
5. P. 37.
6. *tr.* 156 W: *prius quam infans facinus oculi vescuntur tui.*
7. 3.136–7 W: *Tantalus qui poenas, ob facta nefantia, poenas pendit.* 21.886: ... *dissociata aeque omnia ac nefantia.*
8. The old pres. inf. act. is, of course, *esse.*

Conclusion

The fragments of Livius Andronicus are notable for preserving inherited archaisms, such as the $\bar{a}$-stem genitive singular in -$\bar{a}s$, but this study has shown that there is a surprisingly high degree of innovation within Old Latin. Several features that have been taken as archaisms are demonstrably innovated.

The $i̯o$-stem vocative singulars like *fīlie* do not directly continue an inherited *-$i̯e$, since this had become -$ī$ already in Italic. Rather, -$i̯e$ has been analogically "restored" in Latin (and in Umbrian) by analogy to the o-stems (nom. sg. -o-s : voc. sg. -e : : nom. sg. -$i̯o$-s : voc. sg. X = -$i̯e$).

It has been argued that the third plural present endings -*nunt*(*ur*) began from an archaic paradigm of 'to go' (preserved in *obīnunt*, *prodīnunt*, and *redīnunt*) connected with Lith. *einù* 'go' and/or Hitt. *iyannai-* 'start moving'. But this is unlikely given the restriction of the -*n*- to the third plural in Latin and the limitation of the forms almost exclusively to archaic poetry. The -*nunt*(*ur*) forms are better explained as an inner-Latin development starting, not from -*īnunt*, but from *danunt*, which was created as a by-form of *dant* by the analogy, *situs* : *sinunt* :: *datus* : X = *danunt*.

Hominēs has been emended in *Od.* 33 W to *homōnēs*, the latter often thought to be the older form of the stem (cf. Enn. *homōnem*). But the forms cited as evidence of an Italic $\bar{o}n$-stem (Osc. **humuns** and Umbr. *homonus*) could reflect -$\breve{o}n$- as well as -$\bar{o}n$-. *Homōn*- seems rather to have been analogically created within Latin beside older *homŏn- on the model of a growing number of stems in -$\bar{o}n$-. Therefore it is unnecessary, and probably undesirable, to read *homōnēs* in Livius. Nevertheless, the $\bar{o}n$-stem by-form was an innovation of early Latin.

Finally, it is striking that none of these particular innovations survived; in each case the Classical form is more archaic than what is found in Livius Andronicus.

Appendix: The origin of the Latin adjectives in -*ulentus*

The origin of the adjectives in -*ulentus* is a long-standing problem of Latin morphology. No inherited suffix could have given Latin -*ulentus* directly and therefore most scholars have sought an origin for the formant within Latin itself. Perhaps the best discussion of the type is that of Szemerényi,[1] whose investigation focuses on those of the -*ulentus* adjectives that are attested relatively earlier, before c. 50 AD. This cut-off date is determined by the pattern of the attestations themselves; roughly half are first found before c. 50 AD, after which there seems to have been a period of non-productivity until about the middle of the second century when the other half begin to appear.[2] The earlier attested forms[3] are:

aquilentus 'watery' (?) (Var.)
ancunulentus "-ae feminae menstruo tempore appellantur" (Paul. *Fest*.)
bucculentus 'having fat cheeks' (Pl.)
corpulentus 'of a heavy build of body, corpulent, large' (Pl.+)
esculentus 'suitable for food, eatable; (?) eating-vessels' (Scaev.+)
faeculentus 'full of sediment, thick; cloudy' (Col.+)
fraudulentus 'dishonest, deceitful, fraudulent' (Pl.+)
frustulentus 'full of crumbs or morsels' (Pl.+)
gracilentus 'slender, thin' (Enn.+)
iūrulentus 'containing juice or gravy, stewed' (Var.+)
lōtiolentus 'defiled with urine' (Titin.)

lūculentus 'excellent, splendid, fine' (Pl.+)
lutulentus 'full of mud, muddy, miry' (Pl.+)
macilentus 'thin, lean' (Pl.+)
mustulentus 'full of unfermented wine' (Pl.+)
obstrūdulentus 'that can be swallowed down'[4] (Titin.)
opulentus 'having many possessions, wealthy, opulent' (Pl.+)
pestilentus 'insalubrious, unhealthy'[5]
pisculentus 'teeming with fish; made of fish, fishy' (Pl.+)
posculentus 'drinkable' (Scaev.+)
pulverulentus 'covered with or full of dust, dusty' (Var.+)
pūrulentus 'containing or consisting of much pus, purulent' (Cato+)
rōrulentus 'wet with dew' (Cato+)
sanguinolentus (*-ul-*) 'covered with blood, blood-stained, bloody' (Quad.+)
tēmulentus 'drunken' (Ter.+)
truculentus 'ferocious, aggressive' (Pl.+)
turbulentus 'violently disturbed, stormy, turbulent' (Pl.+)
vīnolentus 'immoderate in one's consumption of wine, intoxicated' (Pl.+)
violentus 'acting with force toward others, violent' (Pl.+)

Szemerényi offers what seems to be now the most generally accepted explanation, namely that *-ulent-* is dissimilated from *-en-ont-*. Before turning to this, however, it may be useful first to discuss briefly the inadequacy of some of the previous attempts to explain *-ulentus*.

Ernout[6] argues that *-ulentus* was an entirely Latin creation made by combining the *-ul-* of the type of adjective exemplified by *crēdulus* 'trusting' and *bibulus* 'drinking, thirsty' with an element *-ento-*. This *-ento-* he proposes to have been extracted from *cruentus* 'bloody'. Leumann[7] had earlier proposed that *cruentus* was responsible for part of *-ulentus*, but it is not clear exactly how. As others have noticed, his proportion, *cruentāre* : *violāre* : : *cruentus* : X, does not yield *violentus*. But Ernout, likewise taking *violentus* as the point of departure for the whole class, hypothesizes an adjective **vi-ulus* of the *crēdulus*-type as the basis of the verb *violāre*. He suggests that the semantic similarity between this **vi-ulus* and *cruentus* could have encouraged the blending of their suffixes to give *violentus*. How likely is it, though, that a single, synchronically unanalyzable word like *cruentus* should be fixed upon as a source of a new suffix for a whole class of derived adjectives? Also, it is not clear what a combination of this suffix *-ento-* and an adjective with the semantics of an agent, like *crēdulus*, would mean. In fact, few of the *-ulentus* adjectives are analyzable as expansions of any sort of adjective; there are only *gracilentus* beside *gracilis* (and *gracilus*) and *truculentus* beside *trux*.

Another objection to this scenario is that *crēdulus* and *bibulus* are deverbatives made from the present stems of *crēdō* and *bibō* respectively, whereas Latin has no stem from which a **vi-ulus* could have been derived. Also, the *crēdulus*-type of adjective is not very common in Latin and not a single verbal stem provides both an adjective of this type in *-ulus* and one in *-ulentus*. In fact, virtually all of the *-ulentus* adjectives, with the exception of *obstrūdulentus* and perhaps *ancunulentus*, would appear to be made to nominal stems in the first place.

The theory of A. Zimmermann[8] takes advantage of the other, much larger, group of Latin words in *-ulo-* < **-e-lo-*, namely the diminutives of the type of *porculus* 'small pig' from *porcus*. He proposes the analogy *gracus* (Lucil., Ter.) : *gracilus* :: *gracentes* (Enn.) : X = *gracilens*. Notice that this explanation requires that the athematic by-forms in *-lens* be the older, which is far from certain, and may even qualify as unlikely.

It may be useful at this point to discuss briefly the evidence in this question of whether *-lens* or *-lentus* represents the earlier inflection.[9] If we consider from what dates the *-lens* forms are actually attested, they certainly seem to be a later development; *violens* first appears in Horace while *violentus* is known from Plautus. Similarly, Plautus uses *opulentus*, but *opulens* is first attested in Sallust. On the other hand, *gracilens* (Laev.) and *gracilentus* (Enn.+) are both found in early authors. And *pestilens* is found as early as Cato, whereas *pestilentus* may not really exist at all, since the only potential instance of it is in the phrase *pestilenta loca*, which is completely ambiguous. The appearance already in Plautus and Terence of the derived adverbs of the type *opulenter*[10] could be taken as further evidence that the *-lens* forms are original. But these adverbs in *-ter* could easily have been analogically created at any time without the prior existence of the athematic adjective. In short, it is not probable that the *-lens* forms are the older. But Zimmermann's analogy is open to a more decisive objection.

If we consider all the *-ulentus* adjectives attested from about 50 AD or earlier, it is striking how few of them actually occur beside diminutives. Beside *faeculentus* (Col.+), there is *faecula* (Lucr.+) and beside *bucculentus* (Pl.), *buccula* is given in one manuscript at Plautus *Truc.* 290.[11] In other cases, however, even when the diminutive exists, it is first attested at a significantly later date than the *-ulentus* adjective which is supposedly derived from it; for example, whereas *frustulentus* and *turbulentus* are known from as early as Plautus, *frustulum* and *turbula* first appear in Apuleius.[12] In favor of a derivation from an earlier diminutive, one could add that *turbella* (Pl.+) is at least as old as *turbulentus*, and likewise *macellus* (Lucil.+) beside *macilentus*. But although, from a historical point of view, diminutives in *-ello-* are the result of essentially a doubling (**-el-el-o*) of the same suffix that gives *-ulo-*, these particular diminutives in *-ello-* do not necessarily presuppose earlier diminutives in *-ulo-* from the same stems. *Turbella*, for example, could have been created analogically from *turba* at any time once the pattern *porc-*, *porcul-*, *porcell-* had become established. There would have been no need for an intermediate *turbula* stage.[13] In still other cases, the diminutive is made in a different way altogether, so beside *corpulentus* we have *corpusculum*, not *corpulum, and beside *pisculentus*, *pisciculus*, not *pisculus.

A special case is *aquilentus*. While it is true that *aquola* or *acula* (Pl.+) is older than *aquilentus*, if this diminutive were the basis for the creation of the adjective, one would have expected *aquolentus or *aculentus. If *aquilentus* is derived from the diminutive, it must have undergone some further modification. But it is not even clear if *aquilentus* has anything to do with *aqua*. The *OLD* gives the definition 'watery', but the only instance of the adjective is in Varro, who uses it to describe the moon.[14] *Aquilentus*, and the other words with the variant *-ilentus*, will be discussed further soon.

In short, *-ulentus* resists all attempts to break it down into a concatenation of one or another of the suffixes in eventual *-ulo-* and an *-ento-* of some origin. Therefore, taking a different approach, Szemerényi came to the conclusion that *-ulent-* is the result of a dissimilation from an inherited **-en-ont-*.[15] His prime example is *opulentus* itself, which he analyzes as a thematized version of an IE **op-en-ont-*, a denominative adjective which could also be the pre-form of Hitt. *ḫappinant-* 'rich'.

Szemerényi's analysis may be questioned at several points. Firstly, Hitt. *ḫappinant-* may in fact be a derivative in *-ont-* from the *r/n*-stem preserved in Hittite,[16] but it could also be the adjective *ḫappina-* 'rich' with an added **-nt-*, a type of expansion process that is well-known in Hittite, as Szemerényi himself mentions.[17] Although this sort of addition to an adjective is common in Hittite, it is—to say the least—not at all a wide-spread phenomenon in Latin.

Secondly, most of the examples given for the dissimilation of sequences of *-n- ... -n-* to *-l- ... -n-* date from the time of Romance (*Bonōnia* → *Bologna*, *Barcinōna* → *Barcelona*, *venēnum* → It. *veleno*, *Sāturnīnus* → Fr. *Saint-Sorlin*), rather than from classical Latin or earlier. Szemerényi also cites as a parallel the name *Capitōlīnus*, which Niedermann[18] proposed to be dissimilated from *Capitōnīnus. At best, this example is ambiguous; it is difficult to see why *Capitōlīnus must be a dissimilation, rather than simply a derivative of *Capitōlium* (which cannot have its *-l-* from such a dissimilation), like *Latīnus* from *Latium*. On the other hand, *lympha*, in one of its meanings at least, is probably from Gk. νύμφη, although it may not have been borrowed directly from Greek into Latin. Even if acceptable, however, as an explanation of *opulentus*, this dissimilation is not convincing as the origin of the entire class, since *opulentus* is the only one of the type for which a reconstruction **-en-ont-* is at all likely. Szemerényi suggests that *turbulentus* may be derived from *turbō, turbinis*, rather than from *turba*, but this example is, of course, completely ambiguous.

Szemerényi did recognize that the main obstacle to any explanation of *-ulentus* is the source of the *-l-*. If it is not from the *crēdulus*-type of adjective, on the one hand, nor from the *porculus*-type of diminutive, on the other, then where did it come from? Let us approach the problem now from a slightly different angle.

Leumann and Ernout had tried to exploit the fact that one *-ulentus* adjective, namely *violentus*, is unique in being connected with a similarly problematic verb, *violō*. But the attempts to derive this verb from a **violus* or **viola* are no more convincing than the proposals to get *violentus* from the same sorts of pre-forms, and for the same reasons. A nominal form in **-lo-*, however, is not a prerequisite for a verb in *-lāre*.

Although the "diminutive" suffix **-e-lo-* originally derived endocentric substantives from substantives, as described above, the resulting *-ulo-* in Latin was extended to adjectival bases as well, including participles, e.g., *ēdentulus*, *valentulus*, and *blandiloquentulus*. Eventually, the *-l-* of this suffix seems to have become synchronically perceived as a mark of diminution in itself. This led to its use in the formation of what are sometimes called "diminutive verbs", although in many cases the diminutive force is no longer perceptible. Historically speaking, these seem ultimately to have the *-l-* of the diminutive nouns, but can be either denominative, like *ustulō* 'singe' (*ambustulātus*, Pl.) from *ustus* 'burnt' and *testilor* (a variant of *testiculor* according to Festus) from *testis*, or deverbative, like *obvāgulō* 'wail at' (*obvāgulātum*, XII Tables) from *vāgiō* 'wail' and *petulans* from *petō*.[19] Therefore, *violō* may be described as a present with the "diminutive" denominative formant **(-e)-lā-* in place of simple **-ā-*. It is unnecessary to presuppose a diminutive noun, which does not survive, as the basis of the verb.

Latin also has another set of *-l-* forms that are of neither the *crēdulus-* nor the *porculus*-type. These are adjectives in which, descriptively speaking, the suffix *-ulo-* is a (presumably diminutivizing) substitute for *-uu̯o-*. In Latin, the suffix *-uu̯o-* makes deverbative adjectives, with active force when the verb is intransitive, as in *occiduus* 'sinking, setting' (lit. 'falling down', cf. *cadō*) and *innocuus* 'harmless, innocent' (lit. 'not harming', cf. *noceō*), but with passive force when the verb is transitive, as in *perspicuus* 'clear, transparent' (lit. 'seen through', cf. *speciō*) and *exiguus* 'meager' (lit. 'forced out', cf. *agō*). Whatever their remoter history, *dēlicuus* 'falling short, failing' (Pl.+) is an adjective of this type and we find beside it *dēliculus* 'imperfect, blemished' (Cato), both clearly derivatives of the intransitive verb (*dē-*)*linquō* 'to fail, be wanting'. But *dēliculus* is at least assumed to have a slightly hypocoristic meaning—the OLD defines it as 'having a (small) blemish'— and certainly looks as if it has been formed by simply replacing *-uu̯o-* with *-ulo-*.

The same process would account for *iaculus* 'used for throwing' (Pl.).[20] One would expect such a deverbative to be made with the same *-uu̯o-* as the examples above. But there is no *iacuus attested, so it would seem to have been replaced completely by the "diminutive" version parallel to *dēliculus*. Likewise, *rēiculus* 'discarded' (Var. *ap.* Non.+) has taken the place of *rēicuus.[21] Thus it seems that the type represented by *dēliculus, iaculus,* and *rēiculus* further exemplifies the spread of *-l-* in its capacity as a synchronic diminutive marker.

Something slightly different, however, is going on with the pair *cernuus* (Lucil+) and *cernulus* (Var.+), both meaning essentially 'with the head inclined'.[22] In this case the *-u̯-* apparently being replaced has another source entirely. *Cernuus* is best explained as a compound **k̑erh₂o-nou̯o-*, of the *foedifragus*-type, with a first member exactly cognate with Av. *sāra-* 'head' and a second member derived from the verb *(ad-)nuō* 'to nod'.[23] Notice that in *cernuus* the *-u̯-* belongs, not to a suffix, but to the verbal root itself. This case shows that the synchronic process was *-uu̯o-* > *-ulo-*, whatever the source of the *-u̯-*.

From alternations like *dēlicuus/dēliculus* and *cernuus/cernulus*, it is possible to get the impression that *-l-* could be substituted for **-u̯-* with little or no apparent difference in meaning. This raises another possibility for the source of the *-l-* of *-ulentus*: what if it is a replacement of a **-u̯-*? On this assumption, the immediate pre-form of *-ulent-* would be **-uu̯ent-*. The next question, therefore, is how is this **-uu̯ent-* to be explained? Whereas *-ulent-* could not be equated with any IE suffix ***-lent-*, thereby causing scholars to try to divide it into an *-ul-* plus an *-ent-*, there is a perfectly good IE suffix **-u̯ent-*.

If *-ulentus* goes back ultimately to an inherited **-u̯ent-*, then the thematization of the suffix must be secondary. Such a thematization of a stem in *-nt-* can, however, be paralled in Latin. Although the details of its reconstruction are quite complicated, *cruentus* 'bloody' is generally agreed to contain an inherited athematic suffix, either **-ont-/*-ent-* or perhaps even **-u̯ent-*, which has here been thematized.[24]

The only extra piece of morphology is the surface *-u-* or *-o-* that comes to precede the *-lent-* resulting from **-u̯ent-*. The few examples of an *-i-* in this position (e.g., *gracilentus*) are demonstrably secondary and will be discussed below. The fact that *-o-* is found following an *-i-*, as in *violentus*, but *-u-* appears in most other environments, suggests that the *-o-* and *-u-* are the regular phonological developments of an original **-e-* or **-o-* in these positions. The only likely candidate is the thematic vowel, which frequently serves to link the two halves of compounds in Latin. Compare also the situation in Greek where an *-o-* has been introduced into precisely this formation during the historic period, giving, for example, αἱματόεις 'bloody' as early as Homer versus Myc. (fem.) *pe-de-we-sa* 'having feet'.[25]

Already in 1905, H. Ehrlich proposed that the *-ulentus* adjectives contained the suffix *-u̯ent-*.[26] Again taking the by-forms in *-lens* to be the older, he set up pre-forms of the type **gracilē-u̯ent-* and **violē-u̯ent-* which could contract to give *gracilens* and *violens*. But, as Szemerényi observed[27], the long *-ē-* preceding the suffix is morphologically inexplicable.

That the *-ulentus* adjectives originated in a dissimilation of *-u̯ent-* to *-lent-* has, in fact, already been suggested by Ribezzo in a review of Stolz-Schmaltz's *Lateinische Grammatik* (5er Aufl. völlig neubearbeitet von Manu Leumann u. J. B. Hofmann [München, 1926]).[28] He gives so few details, however, that Szemerényi dismisses the idea with the terse comment: "Nor can any reason be found why, or how, an original **wīno-went-* should have been dissimilated to *vīnolent-*".[29] I hope I have shown how such a dissimilation could have come about; it only remains, therefore, to explain why.

Even granted that it is possible for an inherited *-u̯-* to be replaced by *-l-* in Latin due to a morphologically conditioned analogy to the alternations described above, we must still ask what would have been the motivation, in this case, to change *-u̯ent-* to *-lent-*? Looking again at the list of relatively early *-ulentus* adjectives, one can hardly help noticing that virtually all of them have roots containing a labial or labio-velar consonant, a *u̯-*diphthong, the vowel *-u-*, or even some combination of these. Of the twenty-nine words in our list, twenty-one have a labial consonant, either visible on the surface or reconstructible for the immediate pre-form, and fourteen a *u*-vowel or *u̯*-diphthong. Fully one-third of the list have two such labial elements. The following list shows the labial elements that could have triggered the dissimilation:

-u̯-: *pulver-, vīn-, vi-*
-ŭ-: *ancun-, bucc-, frust-, lut-, must-, pulver-, truc-, turb-*
-ū-: *iūr-, pūr-*
-u̯-diphthongs (or developments thereof): *fraud-, lōti-* (**lau̯t-*), *lūc-* (**leu k̂-*), *obstrūd-*
labio-velars (or reflexes thereof): *aqu-, sanguin-, corp-* (**k^{u}orp-* < **k^{u}r̥p-*, cf. Gk. πρέπει), *ancun-* (if connected with *inquinō*; see E-M)
-p-: *corp-, op-, pest-, pisc-, posc-, pulver-, pūr-*
-b-: *bucc-, obstrūd-, turb-*
-f-: *faec-, fraud-, frust-*
-m-: *mac-, must-, tēm-*.

The exceptions are very few (*esculentus, gracilentus,* and *rōrulentus*) and mostly easily explicable, as we shall see momentarily. This is almost certainly not a coincidence. A suffix *-u̯ent-, added to such a quantity of labial sounds, would surely have made these words likely candidates for a dissimilation.

That a velar -l- should be an acceptable substitute for *-u̯- is not too surprising, given that in Latin these two sounds pattern together in certain ways. Like -u̯-, the *l-pinguis* causes what might be called rounding effects. It is a general rule of Latin that eu̯ > ou̯ and (even though it may be a later change) el > ol in all syllables. Also, in medial syllables, -u̯- and *l-pinguis* are the only two consonants before which a short vowel is regularly reduced to a -u-, e.g., *praesulis*, etc. (< *-sal-, cf. *salio*), *dēpuviō* (< *-păv-, cf. *pavio*).

Typologically, this is as likely a dissimilation as -n- ... -n- to -l- ... -n-. The affinity between -u̯- and -l- seems to be paralleled in Umbrian, which shows a change of *-l- > -u̯- in, for example, **Vuvcis** '*Lucius*' and **vutu** '*lavatō*'.[30] In the Cretan dialect of Greek it is not uncommon to find -υ- for -λ-, as in ἀδευπιαί for ἀδελφεαί and καυχός for καλχός.[31] We might also compare the development of -l- to -u- in, for example, Fr. *autre* from Lat. *alter*. Therefore, if a -u̯- should undergo dissimilation at all, a velar -l- is a very likely outcome.

The instances of -i- preceding the -l- would, therefore, have to have been secondarily altered. In fact, it can be shown that there is a fairly obvious source for the -i- in each of these words. *Gracilentus* could simply have adopted the -i- from its synonym *gracilis*, and *macilentus*, with its very similar meaning, could in turn be modeled on *gracilentus*, although *maciēs* may also have had some influence.[32] *Pestis* and *pestilitās* may well have played a role in creating *pestilens*.

Aquilentus, however, is more problematic. It is used only by Varro to describe the moon and so it is difficult to tell what exactly it means. The usual gloss 'watery' is based on the assumption that it is derived from *aqua*. If this is the right meaning, and if *aquilus* 'dark' is somehow derived from *aqua* also, then the -i- may be from *aquilus*, although it would be irregular there too. The -i- may also be from *aquilus*, whatever its etymology, if we are willing to entertain the idea that *aquilentus* means something like 'dark' as well. But the relationship, if any, between these words has not yet been satisfactorily explained.

To summarize, I would propose, as did Ribezzo, that in the first instance, perhaps in only a few words such as *u̯ī-o-u̯ent-o- and *u̯oi̯no-u̯ent-o-, the occurrence of the two -u̯- sounds in rapid succession motivated a dissimilatory treatment. With a dissimilation thus motivated, the question was how exactly to differentiate one of the -u̯-'s. To accomplish this, advantage was taken of the fact that elsewhere -l-, ultimately traceable to the diminutive suffix, appeared to alternate synchronically with -u̯-, without necessarily conveying a strong diminutive sense, as in *cernuus/cernulus*, etc.

The "new" suffix *-olento- thus created then spread to other stems where the accumulation of labials may have been considered excessive. In fact, this suffix may even be said to have favored stems characterized by labial elements in its initial period of productivity. I do not mean to deny that the suffix has spread to a considerable extent through the semantic similarities (such as in the group *vīnolentus, tēmulentus, mustulentus, posculentus*) noticed by Leumann and others.[33] In fact, this approach can explain the few instances where there was no problematic labial element; *esculentus* is only attested paired with *posculentus* and may easily be modeled on it, and *gracilentus* is synonymous with *macilentus*. The only real exception among the early forms is *rōrulentus*. Of course, *-ulentus* eventually becomes quite productive and the spread to stems without labials had to begin somewhere. But it is surely significant that this is the only such stem we know to have made an *-ulentus* adjective until the end of the first century AD.

Finally, if *-lent-* is really the treatment of *-u̯ent-* in these adjectives, we would have evidence that this familiar IE possessive suffix existed in Latin. Hence this theory has the additional advantage of answering the question of where the potential examples of *-u̯ent-* went.

NOTES

1. "The Latin Adjectives in *-ulentus*" (*Glotta* 33 [1954] p. 266 ff.).
2. Szemerényi, *op. cit.*, p. 266–8.
3. Definitions are from the *OLD*, unless otherwise stated.
4. This is the definition of Lewis and Short; the *OLD* simply refers to the citation.
5. This is only cited, however, in the phrase *pestilenta loca*, Laev. *ap.* Gell., so perhaps only *pestilens* (Cato+) exists.
6. *Les adjectifs latins en -ōsus et en -ulentus* (Paris, 1949) p. 89 f.
7. This theory seems to have disappeared from later editions of L-H; Szemerényi gives the reference as L-H 229.
8. "Zu latein. Suffixen: 1. *-u(i)lentus*. 2. *-os(s)us*" (*KZ* 44 [1911] p.13 ff.).
9. The by-forms in *-lens* are: *gracilens* (Laev.), *opulens* (Sall.), *pestilens* (Cato+), and *violens* (Hor.+).
10. Those that are attested reasonably early are: *fraudulenter* (Cato+), *tēmulenter* (Col.), *lūculenter* (Cic.), *turbulenter* (Cic.), *opulenter* (Pl.+), *violenter* (Ter.+).
11. *Bucculus* also seems to be the title of a play by Novius (see Non. p. 507 M.).
12. A similar case is that of *lūculentus*, which is Plautine, while the adverb *antelūculō* appears first in Apuleius.
13. As mentioned above, *turbula* is found, but only considerably later and may not have been created much before then. Beside *macellus* there seems to be no **maculus* or **macilus* at all. (*Macula* 'stain, spot' and *macilis* 'dappled, piebald' do not fit semantically with *macilentus* and are probably unrelated to it.)
14. *Men.* 400. Lewis and Short interpret *aquilentus* as meaning 'bringing rain'.
15. *Op. cit.*, p. 275 ff.
16. For a fuller discussion of the Hittite forms, see the comment on *ops* above.
17. *Op. cit.*, p. 277. Cf. *assu-/lassuwant-* 'good', *irmala-/irmalant-* 'ill'.
18. *Mél. Ernout* (1940) p. 267 f.

19. Compare also the verbs in -*culo(r)* (*gesticulor*, etc.) and -*illo(r)* (*conscribillō*, etc.). See further L-H, § 414.4.
20. For this development of the passive meaning regular for transitive verbs, compare *pascuus* 'used for feeding' and *caeduus* 'suitable, ready for felling'.
21. This adjective is also used in a substantivized feminine form to mean 'a ewe or other animal culled out of a flock or herd on account of old age, etc.' (*OLD*).
22. Compare also *cernulāre* 'to throw headlong', clearly a factitive of the *(re)novāre*-type from the latter adjective.
23. Nussbaum, p. 114.
24. See also Szemerényi, *op. cit.*, p. 279.
25. That is, *pedwessa* < *-u̯eti̯a*; the consonant cluster -*dw*- is split between two syllabograms, the vowel of the first being a "dummy" determined by the vowel following the cluster. In Indo-Iranian and Hittite, the suffix is also added directly to the stem, e.g., Skt. *padvant-* 'having feet', Hitt. ḫuiṣu̯ant- 'having life, alive'; this was no doubt the inherited situation.
26. "Die nomina auf -ευς" (*KZ* 38 [1905] p. 53 ff.).
27. *Op. cit.*, p. 273.
28. *RIGI* 10 (1926), p. 293 ff.
29. *Op. cit.*, p. 274.
30. See Buck *OU*, § 104, and Untermann, p. 866 f.
31. See Buck *GD*, § 71. Thanks are due to Nina Loney for reminding me of the Cretan facts.
32. Watkins has pointed out that *macilentus* has an interesting correspondent in Hitt. *maklant* 'thin' ("Hittite and Indo-European Studies: the denominative statives in -*ē*-" *Transactions of the Philological Society* [1971], p. 87).
33. See Szemerényi (*op. cit.*, p. 269) with references.

Bibliography

Bader, F. *La formation des composés nominaux du Latin* (Paris, 1962)
Buck, C. G. Buck, C. D. *Comparative Grammar of Greek and Latin* (Chicago, 1933)
Buck, O. U. Buck, C. D. *A Grammar of Oscan and Umbrian*² (Boston, 1928)
Buck, G. D. Buck, C. D. *The Greek Dialects*² (Chicago, 1955)
Buechner, C., ed. *Fragmenta poetarum Latinorum epicorum et lyricorum praeter Ennium et Lucilium* (Leipzig, 1982)
Chantraine, P. *Grammaire homérique* (Paris, 1948 ff.)
De Vries, J. *Altnordisches etymologisches Wörterbuch* (Leiden, 1961)
E-M. Ernout, A. and A. Meillet. Dictionnaire étymologique de la langue latine. *Histoire des mots* (Paris, 1959)
Evans, D. S. *A Grammar of Middle Welsh* (Dublin, 1964)
Feist, S. *Etymologisches Wörterbuch der Gotischen Sprache* (Leiden, 1909)
Flobert, P. *Recherches sur les verbes déponents latins* (diss. Paris, 1973)
Fraenkel, E. *Litauisches etymologisches Wörterbuch* (Heidelberg–Göttingen, 1962)
Frisk, H. *Griechisches etymologisches Wörterbuch* (Heidelberg, 1960)
Geldner, K. *Der Rig-Veda* (Cambridge, MA–London–Leipzig, 1951)
Grassmann, H. *Wörterbuch zum Rig-Veda* (Wiesbaden, 1955)
Huld, M. *Basic Albanian Etymologies* (Columbus, OH, 1984)
Jasanoff, J. *Stative and Middle in Indo-European* (Innsbruck, 1978)
Jocelyn, H. D., ed. *The Tragedies of Ennius* (Cambridge, 1967)
Keller, O. *Lateinisches Volksetymologie* (Leipzig, 1891)
Klingenschmitt, G. *Das Altarmenische Verbum* (Wiesbaden, 1982)

Kronasser, H. *Etymologie der Hethitischen Sprache* (Wiesbaden, 1966)
Lebek, W. D. *Verba Prisca* (Göttingen, 1970)
L-H. Leumann, M. and J. B. Hofmann. *Lateinische Grammatik*[5] (München, 1977)
Lewis, H. and H. Pedersen. *A Concise Comparative Celtic Grammar* (Göttingen, 1937)
LSJ. Liddell, H. and R. Scott, H. Jones, R. McKenzie. *A Greek–English Lexicon* (Oxford, 1961)
Lindsay, W. *Early Latin Verse* (Oxford, 1922)
Lindsay, W., ed. *Nonii Marcelli de compendiosa doctrina* (Leipzig, 1903)
Lindsay, W., ed. *Sexti Pompeii Festi de verborum significatu quae supersunt cum Pauli epitome* (Leipzig, 1913)
Marinetti, A. *Le iscrizioni sudpicene I: testi* (Firenze, 1985)
Mariotti, S. *Livio Andronico e la traduzione artistica* (Milan, 1952)
Meiser, G. *Lautgeschichte der Umbrischen Sprache* (Innsbruck, 1986)
Meister, R. *Die griechischen Dialekte* (Göttingen, 1882–1889)
Melchert, H. C. *Anatolian Historical Phonology* (Amsterdam, 1994)
Meyer-Lübke, W. *Romanisches etymologisches Wörterbuch* (Heidelberg, 1935)
Monier-Williams, M. *Sanskrit–English Dictionary* (Oxford, 1899)
Morel, W., ed. *Fragmenta poetarum Latinorum epicorum et lyricorum praeter Ennium et Lucilium* (Leipzig, 1963)
Nussbaum, A. *Head and Horn in Indo-European* (Berlin–New York, 1986)
OLD. *Oxford Latin Dictionary* (Oxford, 1982)
Pauly-Wissowa. *Real-Enzyclopädie der classischen Altertumswissenschaft* (Stuttgart, 1894 ff.)
Pedersen, H. *Vergleichende Grammatik der Keltischen Sprachen* (Göttingen, 1909)
Peter, H., ed. *Historicorum Romanorum fragmenta* (Leipzig, 1914)
Pokorny, J. *Indogermanisches etymologisches Wörterbuch* (Bern–München, 1959, 1969)
Ribbeck, O., ed. *Scaenicae Romanorum poesis fragmenta* (Leipzig, 1897)
Risch, E. *Wortbildung der homerischen Sprache* (Berlin–Leipzig, 1937)
Rix, H. *Historische Grammatik des Griechischen* (Darmstadt, 1976)
Schmid, W. *Studien zum Baltischen und Indogermanischen Verbum* (Weisbaden, 1963)
Schwyzer, E. *Griechische Grammatik* (München, 1939 ff.)
Sihler, A. L. *New Comparative Grammar of Greek and Latin* (Oxford, 1995)
Skutch, O., ed. *The Annals of Q. Ennius* (Oxford, 1985)
Sommer, F. *Handbuch der Lateinischen Laut- und Formenlehre* (Heidelberg, 1902)
Stowasser, J. M. *Das Verbum LARE* (Vienna, 1892)
TLL. *Thesaurus Linguae Latinae* (Leipzig, 1900 ff.)
Thumb, A. and E. Kieckers. *Handbuch der griechiscen Dialekte*[2] (Heidelberg, 1932–59)
Thurneysen, R. *A Grammar of Old Irish*. tr. D. A. Binchy and O. Bergin (Dublin, 1946)
Tischler, J. *Hethitisches etymologisches Glossar* (Innsbruck, 1977)
Untermann, J. *Wörterbuch des Oskisch-Umbrischen* (Heidelberg, 2000)
Vetter, E. *Handbuch der italischen Dialekte* (Heidelberg, 1953)
Vine, B. *Studies in Archaic Latin Inscriptions* (Innsbruck, 1993)
Wackernagal, J. and A. Debrunner. *Altindische Grammatik* (Göttingen, 1896–1954)
Walde, A. *Lateinisches etymologisches Wörterbuch*. 3. Aufl. von J. B. Hofmann (Heidelberg, 1938)
Warmington, E. *Remains of Old Latin*, vol. 1–3 (London–Cambridge, MA, 1936)

General Index

adverbs in *-per*, 17–21

"*alacer*" rule, 11n7

caesura Korschiana, 43–44

diminutives, 64–65, 75–77

Homer, 7, 9, 43, 51, 78

Livius Andronicus,
    life and works, xi–xiii

meter, xiii–xiv, 15, 43–44

nominal morphology
    ablative sg., *-d*, 64
    adjectives in *-uus*, 10, 77–78
    dative-ablative pl., *-ābus*, 43–44
    genitive sg., *-ās*, 23
    i-stem substantives from *o*-stem adjectives, 10
    o-stem adjectives from *u*-stem substantives, 10
    verbal nouns in *-a*, 50–52
    vocative sg., *-ie*, 5–6, 71

Osthoff's Law, 20, 54

"Sabine *-l-*", 64

verbal morphology
    causative/iterative, 7–8, 23, 29, 34
    "double nasal," 47–50
    $-i^{e}/_{o}$- in Greek and Indo-Iranian, 8–9, 37
    "stative *-ē-*", 8–9, 26–29

Index Verborum

Albanian
    gjej, gjëndem, 48

Armenian
    gtane, 49–50
    harc'ane, 49–50
    lizane, 49
    lk'ane, 49–50
    mah, marh, 10

Avestan
    afnahvant-, 57
    (fra) manyeinte, 8, 38n4
    sāra-, 78

French
    autre, 80
    onze, 22n10, 56n32
    prendre, 54
    prêt, 63
    Saint-Sorlin, 76

Gothic
    aþþan, 56n23
    (bi-, du-)ginnan, 47–48
    guma, 32
    malan, 55n19
    munþs, 41
    sim(b)lē, 19

Greek
    ἀδελφεαί, 80
    ἀδευπιαί, 80
    αἱματόεις, 78
    ἀλάομαι, 65
    ἄκρις, 11n16
    ἄκρος, 11n16
    ἄμβροτος, 9
    ἀντολαί, 51
    ἀοιδή, 51
    ἀπεστύς, 64
    ἀτάρ, 56n23
    Βρόμιε, 6n2
    γαθέω/γηθέω, 37
    γαίω, 37
    δαήρ, 64
    δολιχός, 37
    ἕν, 19
    ἐπαοιδή, 51
    ἐρυθρός, 39
    καλχός, 80
    κάμνω, 49
    καυχός, 80
    κόνις, 35n24
    κυκκέων, 27, 30n18
    λαγχάνω, 49
    λαμβάνω, 49
    λανθάνω, 49
    λείπω, 49
    λιμπάνω, 49–50
    λύω, 39
    μανθάνω, 49
    μασάομαι, 41
    μείρομαι, 8–11, 38n4
    μοῖρα, 7–11
    Μνήμοσυνη, 23, 29
    νεφρός, 67
    νύ, νῦν, 20
    νύμφη, 76
    ὄκρις, 11n16
    ὁμαλός, 36n25
    ὁμός, 36n25

πεδίον, 11n18
πεζός, 11n18
πελιός/πολιός, 39
πέρυσι, 53
περυσινός, 53
πηρός, 59n6
πῆρος, 59n6
πίσυρες, 11n14
προδοχή, 51
προχέω, 51–52
προχοή, 51–52
πυνθάνομαι, 49
σκαι(ϝ)ός, 53
στέλλω, 62
στόλος, 62
συνοχή, 51–52
τάχα, 22n14
ταχύς, 22n14
τυγχάνω, 49
χανδάνω, 47–50
χέω, 51–2
χθών, 32
χοή, 51–52

Greek, Mycenaean
  pe-de-we-sa, 78
  po-ri-wa, 39

Hittite
  assu-, 81n17
  assuwant-, 81n17
  daluka-, 37
  ḫant, 57
  ḫappar, 57–59
  ḫapparai-, 57–59
  ḫappina-, 57–59, 76
  ḫappinaḫḫ-, 57–59
  ḫappinant-, 57–59, 76
  ḫappineš-, 57–59
  ḫappir(iy)a-, 57–59
  ḫuisuant-, 82n25
  irmala-, 81n17
  irmalant, 81n17
  iyannai-, 13, 71
  maklant-, 82n32
  tekan, 32

Italian
  Bologna, 76
  presto, 63
  veleno, 76

Latin
  abavus, 52
  -ābus, 43–44
    ambābus, 43
    dextrābus, 43–44
    duābus, 43
    filiābus, 43
  aceō, 26
  acidus, 27
  acula, 76
  adāgium, 51
  adeō, 65
  adfatim, 10
  adplūda, 55n20
  aēnus, 56n31
  aēs, 56n31
  aestus, 10
  agō, 77
  alia, 53 (see also aliās, under -ās)
  aliēnus, 53
  alter, 80
  ambāgēs, 55n17
  ambō, see ambābus, under -ābus
  ambulo, 65–66
  ambustulātus, 77
  antelūculō, 81n12
  aperiō, 9–10
  applūda, 52

Index Verborum

aqua, 76, 80
aquilus, 80
aquola, 76
arefaciō, 29
areō, 29
arvum, 9
-ās (genitive singular), 23
   aliās, 23, 53
   escās, 23
   familiās, 23
   fortunās, 23
   Latonās, 23
   Monētās, 23, 28–29
   terrās, 23
   viās, 23
aspellō, 55n20
asportō, 55n20
at, 52
atavus, 52
atque, 56n23
atquī, 56n23
audeō, 37–38
autem, 64
autumō, 64
aveō, xv, 38n3
avidus, 37
Barcinōna, 76
bel(u)va, 39
bibō, 75
bibulus, 74–75
bīgae, 6
blandiloquentulus, 77
Bonōnia, 76
Bromie, 6n2
būcītum, 29n14
buccula, 75
cadō, 10, 77
caeduus, 82n20
calefaciō, 29
caleō, 29

Capitōlinus, 76
Capitōlium, 76
carnis (nom. sg.), 66n18
carō, 66n18
caupō, 63
caupōnā, 63
cernō, 14, 16n14
cernulō, 82n22
cernulus, 78, 80
cernuus, 78, 80
certus, 14, 16n14
cinis, 35n24
clam, 64
clanculum, 64
commonēfaciō, 29
compāgēs, 55n17
condocēfaciō, 29
contāgium, 55n17
convertuit, 41
corpusculus, 76
crēdō, 75
crēdulus, 74–75
cruentus, 74, 78
dedro, 16n9
dedron, 13, 16n9
dēliculus, 77–78
dēlicuus, 77–78
dēlinquō, 77
dēplūmis, 68
dēprans, 68
dēpuviō, 80
dexter, 43–44
dingua, 64
doceō, 29
dō, 13–16, 71
dōnō, 14
duō, 43
ēdentulus, 77
edō, 68
ēmineō, 41

epula(e), epulum, xv, 58–59
-ēta, -ētum, xiv, 23–29
    acētum, 25–27, 29
    aesculētum, 23
    arborētum, 23
    asprētum, 25–26
    būcētum, 25–26, 28
    buxētum, 24
    castan(i)ētum, 24
    cocētum, 25, 27
    cornētum, 24
    corylētum, 24
    cupressētum, 23–24
    dūmētum, 24, 28
    fīcētum, 24, 27–28
    fūnētum, 25, 28
    fimētum, 25
    fruticētum, 24, 28
    (h)arundinētum, 24
    īlicētum, 24, 28
    iuncētum, 24, 28
    mālētum, 24
    masculētum, 25, 28
    Monētās, 23, 28–29
    morētum, 25, 27
    myrtēta, 24
    myrtētum (mur-), 24
    nucētum, 24, 28
    olētum ('excrement'), 25–27
    olētum ('olive-yard'), 24
    olīvēta, 25–26
    olīvētum, 24, 26
    olenticētum, 25, 27
    palmētum, 24
    pīnētum, 24
    pōmētum, 24
    pōpulētum, 24
    porculētum, 25, 26
    querquētum (querc-), 24, 28
    rosētum, 24, 28
    rubēta, 25–29
    rubētum, 24, 28
    rumpotinētum, 24
    sabulētum, 24, 26
    salictētum, 24
    saxētum, 24, 26
    senticētum, 24, 28
    sepulcrētum, 24, 26
    spīnētum, 24, 28
    tēmētum, 25–26
    tuccētum, 25–27
    vīminētum, 24
    vīnētum, 24, 28
    veterētum, 25–26
    virgētum, 24
-ētūdō, 30n31
exiguus, 77
facul, 34
faecula, 75
fatuus, 10
ferō, 61–62
fīlia, 43
fīlius, 5–6, 71
flāvus, 39n1
foedifragus, 58
foedus, 58
fossa, 9
fraudulenter, 81n10
(in-)frendo, 67
frūgis, 59n4
frustulum, 75
frux, 59n4
furvus, 39n1
gaudeō, 37–38
gavīsī, 37–38
gracentēs, 75
gracilens, 75, 79, 81n9
gracilis, 74, 80

Index Verborum

gracilus, 74–75
gracus, 75
GNAIVOD, 56n24
hemō, 32–34
homō, xiv, 31–35, 71
homon-, 31–35, 71
homullus, 6, 35n2
horreō, 9, 38n4
iaculus, 78
incipiō, 55n4
infans, 68
inmulgeō, 68–69
inops, 59n3
-issimus, 33
istud, 21
iugum, 6
iungō, 6, 55n6
labrum, 68
lac, 69
Laertius, 5–6
laniēna, 56n30
Lātīnus, 56n30, 76
Lātium, 56n30, 76
lēvir, 64
lībripens, 68
lingua, 64
lūculenter, 81n10
luō, 39
lympha, 76
macellus, 75
maciēs, 80
macilis, 81n13
macula, 81n13
mandō, xv, 41–42
maneō, 8, 38n4
manus, 43
medeor, 8
meminī, 23
Memōria, memōria, 23, 29n7
mentum, 41

mereor, 7–9, 38n4
mihi, 56n33
mil(u)us, 39
moderō, 8
modestus, 8
modus, 8
mola, 52
moneō, 23, 28–29, 34
mons, 41
morior, 9–10
mors, 9–10
Morta, 7–11
mulleus, 39
mundus, 58
nanciō, 53
ne, 34, 36n27
nec, 64
nefandus, 68
nefans, 68
nefās, 67
nefrens, 67–68
nefrōnēs, 67
nefrundinēs, 67
negō, 64
nēmō, 34, 67
nequeō, 15
nesciō, 67
nex, 57
noceō, 77
-nont, -nunt, 13–16
    danunt, 13–16, 71
    explēnunt, 13–16
    ferīnunt, 13–16
    inserinuntur, 13–16
    nequīnont, 13–16
    obīnunt, 13, 15, 71
    prodīnunt, 13, 15, 71
    redīnunt, 13, 15, 71
(rē-)novō, 66n15, 82n22
nudius tertius, 20

(ad-)nuō, 78
nullus, 36n26
nunc, 20
obscēnus, 53
obvāgulātum, 77
occiduus, 10, 77
odor, 64
olea, 69
oleō, 26, 64
olidus, 27
olīva, 69
Opis, 59n4
opitulor, 58–59
opitulus, 58–59
ops, Ops, xv, 57–59
opulens, 75, 81n9
opulenter, 75, 81n10
opulentus, 76
opus, xv, 58–59
palleō, 39
pallidus, 39
pallor, 39
pālor, 65–66
parum, 21n3
pascuus, 82n20
paviō, 80
pel(u)vis, 39
Pellaeō, 53
pendō, 68
-per, 17–22
    aliquantisper, 19
    nūper, 18–19
    parumper, 18–19
    paul(l)isper, 18–19
    paul(l)umper, 18–19
    pauxillisper, 19–20
    quantisper, 19
    semper, 18–19
    tantisper, 19
    topper, 17–22

perspicuus, 10, 77
pestilens, 75, 80, 81n9
pestilitās, 80
pestis, 80
petō, 77
petulans, 77
pisciculus, 76
plaudō, 52
pleō, 15
poc(u)lum, 61
pondus, 58
porcellus, 76
porcus, 75–76
porculus, 75–76
praebeō, 50
praebia, 55n16
praeda, xiv, 47, 50–54
praehibeō, 55n16
praemium, 51
praendō, 53–54
praeolō, 53
praesens, 63
praeses, 68
praesideō, 68
praesidium, 68
praestō (adv.), 61–66
praestō (perf. praestāvī), 66n15
praestō (perf. praestitī), 66n15
praestōlo(r), xiv, 61–66
praestū, 63–64
praesulis, 80
praetor, 50–51
praeustis, 53
praeut, 53
prandium, 68
prandō, 68
(com-, dē-) pre(he)ndō,
    36n26, 47–48, 52–54
promptū, 63
pullus, 38–39

quattuor, 10
quō (adv.), 65
quoad, 65
rāvis, 19
rāvus, 19
reguit, 41
rēgula, 58
rēiculus, 78
remora, 52
remoror, 52
rota, 52
rubeō, 26, 28, 36n29
ruber, 39
rūbidus, 27
rubus, 28
saliō, 80
Sāturnīnus, 76
scaevus, 53
sēcēdō, 52
secta, 9
sēcūrus, 52
sēdulō, 66n14
sēdulus, 66n14
semel, 19
similis, 33
simul, 19, 33–34
sinō, 14–16, 71
solinō, 15, 16n6
solinunt, 13–16
solvō, 39
speciō, 10, 77
st, 33
strāgulum, 58
sum, 33
taceō, 27
tam, 21
tegō, 52
tēmulenter, 81n10
terra, 56n31
terrēnus, 56n31

testiculor, 77
testilor, 77
testis, 77
tībīcen, 6
toga, 52, 54
tollō, 58
topper, see -per
trux, 74
tum, 21
tunc, 22n12
turba, 76–77
turbella, 75
turbō, 77
turbula, 75
turbulenter, 81n10
ūber, 68–69
-ulentus, xiv, 73–82
    aquilentus, 73, 76, 79–80
    ancunulentus, 73, 75, 79
    bucculentus, 73, 75, 79
    corpulentus, 73, 79
    esculentus, 73, 79, 81
    faeculentus, 73, 75, 79
    fraudulentus, 73, 79
    frustulentus, 73, 75, 79
    gracilentus, 73, 78, 79–81
    iūrulentus, 73, 79
    lōtiolentus, 73, 79
    lūculentus, 74, 79, 81n12
    lutulentus, 74, 79
    macilentus, 74–75, 79–81
    mustulentus, 74, 79, 81
    obstrūdulentus, 74–75, 79
    opulentus, 74–76, 79
    pestilentus, 74–75, 79
    pisculentus, 74, 79
    posculentus, 74, 79, 81
    pulverulentus, 74, 79
    pūrulentus, 74, 79
    rōrulentus, 74, 79, 81

sanguinolentus (-ul-), 74, 79
tēmulentus, 74, 79, 81
truculentus, 74, 79
turbulentus, 74–75, 79
vīnolentus, 74, 79, 81
violentus, 74–75, 77–79
undecim, 22n10, 56n32
ustulō, 77
ustus, 77
vāgiō, 77
valentulus, 77
vegeō, 8
vehis, 59n4
venēnum, 76
vīcīnus, 53
vīcus, 53
videō, 38
violens, 79, 81n9
violenter, 81n10
violō, 64, 74, 77
virgō, 32
vīs, 64

Lithuanian
diẽvo, 56n24
einù, 13, 71
mulvas, 39
paĺvas, 39
žmuõ, 32

Lycian
epirijeti, 57–58
xñtawa-, 57

Middle Welsh
genni, 47–48
hynhaf, 33
mant, 41

Old English
fealo, 39
(be-, for-)geitan, 47–48
(bi-, on-)ginnan, 47–48
guma, 32
mūð, 41
rudu, 30n29
sím(b)les, 19

Old High German
uoba, 58
uoben, 58

Old Irish
aith-, 56n23
marb, 9
melid, 52
rethid, 52
ro-geinn, 47–49
sinem, 33
tír, 56n31

Old Norse
fǫlr, 39
geta, 47–48
muðr, 41

Old Church Slavonic
mritvŭ, 9

Oscan
destrst, 33
eituas, 23
humuns, 31–32, 34, 71
leginei, **leginum**, 6
meddíss, **medíkeís**, 31
pertiro-pert, 19
sakruvit, 5
súm, 33

statie, xiii
tanginom, 6
úíttiuf, 6n3

Sanskrit
ápas, 58
ā́pas, xv, 58
apnas-, 57
ā́pra-, 58
apṛcchat, 49
áśri-, 11n16
ávati, xv, 38n3
avidat, 49
bhanakti, 55n5
devar-, 64
devā́t, 56n24
hṛ́ṣyati, 9, 38n4
jmán, 32–33
kṣami, 33
mṛta-, 9
nu, nū, 20
padvant-, 82n25
rudhira-, 39
smarate, 29n7
tapana-, 57
vindati, 49
yunakti, 55n6

South Picene
méfistrúi, 31
meitimúm, 35n8
nemúneí, 31–32, 34
safinús, 35n8

Spanish
Barcelona, 76

Tocharian
kātk-, 38n5

Umbrian
amparitu, xiii
heri, heris, xiii, 5
homonus, 31–34, 71
maletu, 31
mehe, 56n33
natine, 6
taçez, 27
tasetur, 31
triiu-per, 19
tutas, 23
sumul, 33–34, 36n25
Vuvcis, 80
vutu, 80

For Product Safety Concerns and Information please contact our EU representative GPSR@taylorandfrancis.com
Taylor & Francis Verlag GmbH, Kaufingerstraße 24, 80331 München, Germany

www.ingramcontent.com/pod-product-compliance
Lightning Source LLC
Chambersburg PA
CBHW052133300426
44116CB00010B/1886